Table of Contents

11

19

Chapter 1: Mastering Advanced CryEngine Features

1.1. Exploring Deep Features of CryEngine

In this section, we will delve into the intricate and powerful features that CryEngine offers to game developers. CryEngine is renowned for its cutting-edge technology and versatility, making it a preferred choice for creating high-quality games with stunning visuals and immersive gameplay experiences.

CryEngine's deep feature set includes advanced rendering capabilities, robust AI systems, efficient scene management, and extensive customization options. Let's explore some of the key aspects of these features:

1.1.1. Advanced Rendering Techniques

CryEngine provides a wide range of rendering techniques to achieve photorealistic visuals. Developers can harness the power of physically-based rendering (PBR) to simulate the behavior of materials accurately. This involves creating materials with realistic properties such as reflectivity, roughness, and metalness, resulting in stunningly lifelike surfaces.

Here's a code snippet showcasing how to define a PBR material in CryEngine:

```
// Define a PBR material
Material myMaterial;
myMaterial.SetDiffuseColor(Vector3(1.0f, 0.0f, 0.0f)); // Set diffuse color t
o red
myMaterial.SetRoughness(0.2f); // Set roughness value
myMaterial.SetMetalness(0.8f); // Set metalness value
```

1.1.2. Advanced AI Systems

CryEngine's AI systems are highly sophisticated, allowing developers to create intelligent and realistic non-player characters (NPCs). The engine supports behavior trees, finite state machines, and dynamic navigation, enabling NPCs to react intelligently to the game world and player actions.

```
-- Example behavior tree in Lua for an AI character
local behaviorTree = BehaviorTree:new({
    Sequence(
        Selector(
            IsPlayerVisible(),
            Wander()
        ),
        Attack()
    )
})
```

1.1.3. Scene Management and Optimization

Efficient scene management is crucial for maintaining performance in complex game environments. CryEngine offers various tools for optimizing scene rendering, including occlusion culling, LOD (Level of Detail) systems, and efficient resource streaming.

```
// Occlusion culling setup
OcclusionCulling occlusionCulling;
occlusionCulling.Enable(); // Enable occlusion culling
```

1.1.4. Custom Extensions and Plugin Development

To extend CryEngine's functionality, developers can create custom extensions and plugins. This allows for the integration of third-party libraries, tools, and additional features tailored to specific project requirements.

```
// Sample code for creating a custom plugin
class MyCustomPlugin : public CryHooksModule
{
    // Implementation of plugin functionalities
};
CRYREGISTER_SINGLETON_CLASS(MyCustomPlugin)
```

1.1.5. Full Utilization of CryEngine's Capabilities

CryEngine offers a wide array of features, and mastering them opens the door to limitless possibilities in game development. From real-time global illumination to advanced audio systems and powerful scripting support, CryEngine empowers developers to bring their creative visions to life.

In the upcoming sections of this chapter, we will dive deeper into each of these aspects, providing in-depth tutorials, tips, and best practices for harnessing the full potential of CryEngine. Whether you are a seasoned developer or new to CryEngine, this chapter will equip you with the knowledge and skills needed to create exceptional games.

1.2. Advanced Scene Management and Optimization

Advanced scene management and optimization are fundamental aspects of game development when using CryEngine. Efficiently handling the rendering of complex scenes, managing assets, and optimizing performance are essential for delivering a seamless player experience. In this section, we will explore various techniques and tools that CryEngine provides for advanced scene management and optimization.

1.2.1. Occlusion Culling

Occlusion culling is a technique that helps improve rendering performance by avoiding the rendering of objects that are not visible to the camera. CryEngine offers built-in occlusion culling support, allowing developers to define occluder objects in the scene and automatically hide objects that are occluded from the camera's view.

```
// Enabling occlusion culling
OcclusionCulling occlusionCulling;
occlusionCulling.Enable();
```

Developers can also use the CryEngine Editor to set up occluder objects visually, optimizing the culling process further. Properly implementing occlusion culling can significantly reduce the rendering workload and enhance frame rates.

1.2.2. Level of Detail (LOD) Systems

Level of Detail (LOD) systems are crucial for managing the rendering complexity of objects in the game world. CryEngine allows developers to define multiple levels of detail for objects and dynamically switch between them based on the distance from the camera.

```
// Defining LOD levels for a 3D model
Model myModel;
myModel.AddLOD("low", "low_model.obj", 100.0f);
myModel.AddLOD("medium", "medium_model.obj", 50.0f);
myModel.AddLOD("high", "high_model.obj", 0.0f);
```

By using LOD systems effectively, you can ensure that distant objects have lower-polygon representations, reducing the rendering workload without sacrificing visual quality.

1.2.3. Efficient Resource Streaming

Resource streaming is the process of loading game assets dynamically as they are needed, rather than loading everything at once. CryEngine provides a resource streaming system that can be customized to load and unload assets based on various criteria, such as proximity to the player or gameplay events.

```
// Implementing resource streaming for textures
TextureManager textureManager;
textureManager.StreamTexturesInRadius(playerPosition, 1000.0f);
```

Efficient resource streaming ensures that the game utilizes system resources optimally and minimizes loading times during gameplay.

1.2.4. GPU and CPU Optimization

Optimizing both GPU and CPU performance is critical for achieving smooth gameplay. CryEngine offers profiling and debugging tools to identify bottlenecks in your game's performance. By analyzing performance data and using techniques like parallelization and multi-threading, you can maximize hardware utilization.

```
// Profiling GPU performance
ProfilingSystem profilingSystem;
profilingSystem.EnableGPUProfiling();
```

Additionally, CryEngine's Asset Compiler can help optimize game assets, such as textures and models, for better GPU performance.

1.2.5. Advanced Lighting Techniques

Lighting plays a significant role in the visual quality of a game. CryEngine supports advanced lighting techniques like real-time global illumination (GI) and physically-based rendering (PBR) materials. These techniques can create realistic lighting effects and enhance the overall visual appeal of the game.

```
// Enabling real-time global illumination
LightingSystem lightingSystem;
lightingSystem.EnableGlobalIllumination();
```

In this section, we've only scratched the surface of advanced scene management and optimization in CryEngine. Properly implementing these techniques and tools is essential for delivering a high-quality gaming experience while maintaining optimal performance. As you continue to explore CryEngine, you'll discover more in-depth strategies and best practices for scene optimization that will help you create exceptional games.

1.3. Custom Extensions and Plugin Development

Custom extensions and plugin development are powerful ways to extend the functionality of CryEngine to meet the specific needs of your game project. Whether you want to integrate third-party libraries, add new features, or modify existing functionality, CryEngine provides a flexible framework for creating custom extensions and plugins.

1.3.1. Plugin Architecture

CryEngine follows a modular architecture that allows developers to create plugins easily. These plugins can be written in C++ or Lua, making it accessible for both programmers and scripters.

C++ Plugins

To create a C++ plugin, you typically follow these steps:

1. Define a new C++ class that inherits from CRYINTERFACE or CRYPLUGIN.
2. Implement the desired functionality within your class.
3. Register your plugin with the engine using the CRYREGISTER_SINGLETON_CLASS macro.

Here's a simplified example of a C++ plugin that adds a custom weapon to the game:

```
class CustomWeaponPlugin : public CRYINTERFACE
{
```

```
public:
    // Implement custom weapon functionality here
};
```

```
CRYREGISTER_SINGLETON_CLASS(CustomWeaponPlugin)
```

Lua Plugins

Creating Lua plugins is more accessible for scripters. You can define custom Lua functions and scripts to extend the game's functionality dynamically. CryEngine's Lua integration makes it straightforward to create and load Lua plugins.

1.3.2. Integration of Third-Party Libraries

CryEngine allows you to integrate third-party libraries and tools into your project seamlessly. Whether you need physics engines, audio middleware, or specialized AI libraries, CryEngine's extensibility enables you to incorporate these components.

For instance, if you want to integrate a physics engine like NVIDIA PhysX, you can create a custom plugin that bridges CryEngine's physics systems with PhysX.

```
class PhysXIntegrationPlugin : public CRYPLUGIN
{
public:
    // Integrate PhysX physics engine here
};
```

```
CRYREGISTER_SINGLETON_CLASS(PhysXIntegrationPlugin)
```

1.3.3. Extending Editor Functionality

CryEngine's editor can also be extended using custom plugins. This allows you to create specialized tools and workflows that streamline your level design and game development processes. Custom editor plugins can add new UI elements, property panels, and even entirely new editor modes.

```
class CustomEditorPlugin : public CRYPLUGIN
{
public:
    // Extend editor functionality here
};
```

```
CRYREGISTER_SINGLETON_CLASS(CustomEditorPlugin)
```

1.3.4. Modifying Gameplay Logic

Plugins can modify gameplay logic, including AI behavior, player abilities, and game rules. For example, you can create a plugin that introduces new enemy AI behaviors or adds unique player abilities, all without modifying the core engine code.

```
class GameplayModificationPlugin : public CRYPLUGIN
{
public:
    // Modify gameplay logic here
};

CRYREGISTER_SINGLETON_CLASS(GameplayModificationPlugin)
```

1.3.5. Cross-Platform Compatibility

Custom extensions and plugins created for CryEngine can often be reused across different platforms. This flexibility allows you to develop games for various platforms while maintaining a consistent codebase for your custom functionality.

In this section, we've explored the concept of custom extensions and plugin development in CryEngine. These capabilities empower game developers to tailor CryEngine to their specific project requirements, extend its functionality, and integrate external resources seamlessly. Whether you're enhancing editor tools, modifying gameplay, or integrating third-party libraries, custom extensions and plugins are essential tools in your CryEngine toolkit.

1.4. Utilizing CryEngine's Full Rendering Capabilities

CryEngine is renowned for its cutting-edge rendering capabilities, allowing game developers to create visually stunning and immersive worlds. In this section, we will delve into how to utilize CryEngine's full rendering capabilities to achieve exceptional graphics and visual fidelity in your games.

1.4.1. Physically-Based Rendering (PBR)

CryEngine employs Physically-Based Rendering (PBR), a rendering technique that simulates the physical properties of materials and lighting accurately. PBR enables you to create materials that respond realistically to light, resulting in lifelike surfaces. CryEngine's PBR system includes parameters for albedo, roughness, metalness, and more, allowing you to craft materials with incredible detail and realism.

```
// Defining a PBR material in CryEngine
Material myMaterial;
myMaterial.SetDiffuseColor(Vector3(0.8f, 0.8f, 0.8f)); // Set albedo color
myMaterial.SetRoughness(0.2f); // Set roughness value
myMaterial.SetMetalness(0.5f); // Set metalness value
```

1.4.2. Real-Time Global Illumination (GI)

Global Illumination (GI) is a crucial aspect of achieving realistic lighting in games. CryEngine provides real-time GI solutions that calculate indirect lighting in real-time, ensuring that light bounces realistically off surfaces. This creates beautifully lit environments with soft shadows and natural lighting transitions.

```
// Enabling real-time Global Illumination
LightingSystem lightingSystem;
lightingSystem.EnableGlobalIllumination();
```

1.4.3. Advanced Shader Programming

CryEngine supports advanced shader programming, allowing you to create custom shaders to achieve unique visual effects. You can manipulate lighting, materials, and post-processing effects through shader code. This level of control is invaluable for achieving specific artistic goals and enhancing the visual quality of your game.

```
// Example HLSL shader code for a custom post-processing effect
float4 MyCustomPostProcess(float2 texCoord : TEXCOORD) : SV_Target
{
    // Implement custom post-processing effect here
}
```

1.4.4. High-Dynamic-Range Imaging (HDRI)

High-Dynamic-Range Imaging (HDRI) is essential for capturing a broad range of lighting intensities in the game world. CryEngine supports HDR rendering, enabling you to create scenes with bright highlights and deep shadows. This adds depth and realism to the visuals, especially in outdoor environments and scenes with extreme lighting conditions.

```
// Enabling High-Dynamic-Range Imaging (HDRI)
RenderSettings renderSettings;
renderSettings.EnableHDR();
```

1.4.5. Particle Systems and Visual Effect Enhancements

CryEngine offers powerful particle systems and visual effect tools to create dynamic and captivating effects. You can simulate various phenomena such as fire, smoke, explosions, and more. These particle systems are fully integrated with CryEngine's rendering pipeline, ensuring seamless integration into your game.

```
// Creating a particle effect in CryEngine
ParticleEmitter particleEmitter;
particleEmitter.CreateEffect("explosion.pfx");
particleEmitter.Play();
```

1.4.6. Real-Time Rendering Optimization Strategies

While harnessing CryEngine's rendering capabilities is essential for achieving stunning visuals, optimization is equally critical. CryEngine provides various rendering optimization techniques, including LOD (Level of Detail) systems, occlusion culling, and efficient resource streaming. These strategies ensure that your game maintains a high frame rate even in demanding scenes.

In this section, we've explored how to leverage CryEngine's full rendering capabilities to create visually impressive games. Whether it's through PBR materials, real-time global illumination, advanced shaders, HDR imaging, or particle systems, CryEngine equips developers with the tools needed to bring their artistic visions to life with exceptional visual fidelity. Understanding and mastering these rendering capabilities is key to delivering a visually captivating gaming experience.

1.5. Advanced AI Systems and Implementation

In modern game development, creating realistic and intelligent non-player characters (NPCs) is essential to delivering immersive gameplay experiences. CryEngine offers a robust set of tools and features for implementing advanced AI systems that can interact with the game world and the player in sophisticated ways. In this section, we will explore the world of advanced AI systems and their implementation within CryEngine.

1.5.1. Behavior Trees

Behavior trees are a fundamental component of advanced AI systems in CryEngine. These hierarchical structures enable developers to define the decision-making processes of NPCs in a clear and organized manner. Behavior trees consist of nodes that represent different actions, conditions, and tasks that an NPC can perform.

```xml
<!-- Example behavior tree XML definition -->
<BehaviorTree>
    <Selector>
        <Sequence>
            <ConditionNode type="IsEnemyVisible" />
            <ActionNode type="AttackEnemy" />
        </Sequence>
        <ActionNode type="Wander" />
    </Selector>
</BehaviorTree>
```

1.5.2. Finite State Machines (FSM)

Finite State Machines are another vital tool for creating AI behavior in CryEngine. FSMs allow you to model the AI's behavior as a set of discrete states, each with its own set of actions and transitions. This approach is particularly useful for character behaviors with well-defined states, such as combat, idle, and patrolling.

```xml
<!-- Example FSM definition for NPC states -->
<FSM>
    <State name="Idle">
        <Action type="PlayAnimation" name="IdleAnimation" />
        <Transition event="PlayerDetected" targetState="Alert" />
    </State>
```

```
    <State name="Alert">
        <Action type="PlayAnimation" name="AlertAnimation" />
        <Transition event="EnemyInSight" targetState="Attack" />
    </State>
    <!-- More states and transitions defined here -->
</FSM>
```

1.5.3. Dynamic Navigation

CryEngine provides advanced navigation capabilities, allowing NPCs to navigate complex environments dynamically. Dynamic navigation includes pathfinding, avoidance behaviors, and terrain analysis. NPCs can calculate paths around obstacles, avoid collisions, and adapt to changes in the game world.

```
// Implementing dynamic navigation for an NPC
NPCCharacter npc;
npc.EnableDynamicNavigation();
```

1.5.4. AI Debugging and Visualization

Effective AI development involves debugging and visualization tools to understand AI behavior and identify issues. CryEngine offers tools for visualizing behavior trees, FSMs, and navigation paths in real-time. This visual feedback is invaluable for fine-tuning AI behaviors and ensuring they align with your game's design.

```
// Enabling AI debugging and visualization
DebuggingSystem debuggingSystem;
debuggingSystem.EnableAIDebugging();
```

1.5.5. Scripted AI Behaviors

CryEngine also supports scripted AI behaviors through Lua scripting. You can define custom AI logic in Lua scripts, allowing for flexible and dynamic NPC behaviors. Scripted AI can react to specific in-game events, follow complex patterns, and interact with other game systems.

```
-- Example Lua script for scripted AI behavior
function OnPlayerDetected()
    -- Implement behavior when the player is detected
end

function OnEnemyInSight()
    -- Implement behavior when an enemy is in sight
end
```

1.5.6. Learning and Adaptation

Advanced AI systems can incorporate learning and adaptation mechanisms. CryEngine allows developers to create NPCs that can learn from player actions, adapt to changing game conditions, and make decisions based on experience. This level of sophistication enhances the realism and challenge of the gameplay.

In this section, we've delved into the world of advanced AI systems and their implementation within CryEngine. From behavior trees and finite state machines to dynamic navigation, debugging tools, scripted AI behaviors, and learning mechanisms, CryEngine provides a comprehensive toolkit for creating intelligent and lifelike NPCs. Mastering these AI capabilities is essential for developers looking to deliver immersive and engaging gameplay experiences.

Chapter 2: High-Performance Coding Practices

2.1. Efficient C++ and Lua Scripting for Performance

Efficient coding practices are crucial for optimizing the performance of your game in CryEngine. Whether you are writing C++ code for core engine components or Lua scripts for gameplay logic, understanding how to write efficient code can make a significant difference in the overall performance of your game.

2.1.1. C++ Coding Practices

2.1.1.1. Memory Management

Efficient memory management is a key aspect of C++ programming. In CryEngine, developers often deal with managing complex data structures and resource allocation. It's essential to allocate memory judiciously and release resources when they are no longer needed to prevent memory leaks.

```
// Efficient memory allocation in C++
MyObject* object = new MyObject();
```

2.1.1.2. Use of Smart Pointers

C++ smart pointers, such as `std::shared_ptr` and `std::unique_ptr`, help manage memory automatically and reduce the risk of memory leaks. Utilizing smart pointers is a recommended practice when dealing with dynamic memory allocation in CryEngine.

```
// Using smart pointers for memory management
std::shared_ptr<MyObject> object = std::make_shared<MyObject>();
```

2.1.1.3. Minimizing Copy Operations

Avoid unnecessary copy operations, especially for large data structures. Use references or move semantics to reduce the overhead of copying data.

```
// Minimizing copy operations with move semantics
std::vector<int> source = {1, 2, 3};
std::vector<int> destination = std::move(source);
```

2.1.1.4. Profiling and Optimization

Utilize profiling tools and techniques to identify performance bottlenecks in your C++ code. CryEngine provides profiling tools to help you pinpoint areas that require optimization. Optimize critical code paths to improve overall game performance.

```
// Profiling code for optimization
ProfilingSystem profilingSystem;
profilingSystem.EnableProfiling();
```

2.1.2. Lua Scripting Practices

2.1.2.1. Avoid Global Variables

Avoid using global variables in Lua scripts as much as possible. Global variables can lead to naming conflicts and make code harder to maintain. Instead, use local variables and function parameters within the appropriate scope.

```lua
-- Avoid global variables
local myVariable = 10
```

2.1.2.2. Efficient Data Structures

Choose appropriate data structures for your Lua scripts. Lua offers tables, which can be used for various purposes. Use tables efficiently and consider the data access patterns to minimize unnecessary operations.

```lua
-- Efficient use of Lua tables
local myTable = {}
myTable[1] = "Item 1"
myTable[2] = "Item 2"
```

2.1.2.3. Avoid Heavy Computation in Scripts

Avoid performing heavy computational tasks within Lua scripts. Complex calculations are better suited for C++ code, which is typically more efficient. Lua scripts should focus on gameplay logic and scripting interactions.

```lua
-- Avoid heavy computation in Lua scripts
function CalculateDamage()
    -- Perform heavy calculations in C++ instead
end
```

2.1.2.4. Error Handling

Implement robust error handling in Lua scripts to gracefully handle unexpected situations. Proper error handling can prevent script crashes and improve the stability of your game.

```lua
-- Error handling in Lua scripts
local success, result = pcall(function()
    -- Code that might raise an error
end)

if not success then
    Log("Error: " .. result)
end
```

2.1.3. Hybrid C++ and Lua Optimization

CryEngine allows you to combine C++ and Lua scripting for flexibility and performance. You can offload computationally intensive tasks to C++ while using Lua for high-level scripting. This hybrid approach optimizes both performance-critical and gameplay-specific code.

In this section, we've explored efficient coding practices for both C++ and Lua scripting in CryEngine. Optimizing memory management, minimizing copy operations, using smart pointers, avoiding global variables, and practicing error handling are essential techniques to enhance the performance and stability of your game. Mastering these practices is crucial for achieving high performance in CryEngine development.

2.2. Memory Management and Allocation Strategies

Efficient memory management is a critical aspect of high-performance game development in CryEngine. Properly handling memory allocation and deallocation can have a significant impact on the stability and performance of your game. In this section, we will explore memory management strategies and allocation techniques to optimize your CryEngine projects.

2.2.1. Stack vs. Heap Memory

In C++ programming, memory can be allocated on either the stack or the heap. Understanding the differences between stack and heap memory allocation is essential for efficient memory management.

- **Stack Memory**: Stack memory is used for storing local variables with a limited scope. It is automatically allocated and deallocated when a function is called and returns. Stack memory is typically faster to allocate and deallocate than heap memory. However, it has a limited size, and excessive usage can lead to stack overflow errors.

```
void MyFunction()
{
    int localVariable = 42; // Stack memory allocation
}
```

- **Heap Memory**: Heap memory, also known as dynamic memory, is used for objects with a longer lifetime or unknown size. Memory on the heap must be manually allocated and deallocated using functions like new and delete or their C++11 counterparts, malloc and free. Heap memory offers more flexibility but can lead to memory leaks or fragmentation if not managed correctly.

```
int* dynamicVariable = new int(42); // Heap memory allocation
delete dynamicVariable; // Deallocate heap memory
```

2.2.2. Smart Pointers

C++ smart pointers, such as std::shared_ptr and std::unique_ptr, provide automatic memory management, reducing the risk of memory leaks. They are especially valuable when dealing with complex data structures or objects that need to be shared among multiple parts of your code.

```
// Using std::shared_ptr for automatic memory management
std::shared_ptr<int> sharedVariable = std::make_shared<int>(42);
```

2.2.3. Resource Management

Efficiently managing game resources, such as textures, models, and audio files, is crucial for performance. CryEngine provides resource management systems that help load and unload resources dynamically based on demand. Utilize these systems to avoid unnecessary memory consumption.

```
// Resource management in CryEngine
ResourceSystem resourceSystem;
resourceSystem.LoadResource("my_texture.dds");
resourceSystem.UnloadResource("my_texture.dds");
```

2.2.4. Object Pools

Object pools are data structures used to manage and reuse objects efficiently. Instead of constantly allocating and deallocating memory for frequently created and destroyed objects, you can preallocate a pool of objects and reuse them when needed. This reduces the overhead of memory allocation and deallocation.

```
// Object pool for managing game entities
ObjectPool<Entity> entityPool(100); // Create a pool with 100 entities
Entity* newEntity = entityPool.Acquire(); // Get a reusable entity
entityPool.Release(newEntity); // Release the entity back to the pool
```

2.2.5. Memory Profiling

CryEngine provides memory profiling tools to monitor and analyze memory usage during runtime. These tools help you identify memory leaks, excessive memory usage, or fragmentation issues. Regular memory profiling can guide optimizations and ensure efficient memory management.

```
// Enabling memory profiling in CryEngine
ProfilingSystem profilingSystem;
profilingSystem.EnableMemoryProfiling();
```

2.2.6. Custom Memory Allocators

For advanced memory optimization, you can implement custom memory allocators tailored to your game's specific requirements. Custom allocators can minimize memory fragmentation and improve memory locality, leading to better performance.

```
// Custom memory allocator example
void* CustomAllocate(size_t size)
{
    // Implement custom memory allocation logic
```

```
}

void CustomDeallocate(void* memory)
{
    // Implement custom memory deallocation logic
}

// Set the custom allocator for a specific resource type
ResourceSystem::SetCustomAllocator(ResourceType::Texture, CustomAllocate, Cus
tomDeallocate);
```

In conclusion, efficient memory management and allocation strategies are essential for optimizing the performance and stability of your CryEngine games. Whether you're using stack memory, heap memory, smart pointers, object pools, or custom memory allocators, choosing the right approach for each situation and regularly profiling your memory usage are key practices in high-performance game development.

2.3. Multithreading and Concurrent Processing in CryEngine

Multithreading is a fundamental technique in modern game development to harness the power of multi-core processors and improve performance. CryEngine provides robust support for multithreading, allowing developers to parallelize various tasks for more efficient processing. In this section, we will explore the concepts of multithreading and concurrent processing in CryEngine.

2.3.1. Multithreading Basics

Multithreading involves splitting a program into multiple threads of execution that can run concurrently. Each thread performs a specific task, and when used correctly, multithreading can lead to improved performance and responsiveness.

In CryEngine, multithreading can be applied to various aspects of game development, such as physics simulations, rendering, AI computations, and resource loading. By distributing these tasks across multiple threads, you can utilize the full potential of modern CPUs.

2.3.2. CryEngine's Multithreading Model

CryEngine employs a multithreading model that separates the engine's core components into different threads. Here are some key components of CryEngine's multithreading model:

- **Main Thread**: This is the primary thread responsible for handling user input, managing the game's main loop, and updating the game logic. It's also known as the "main thread" or "render thread."

- **Physics Thread**: CryEngine allows you to offload physics simulations to a separate thread. This separation ensures that physics calculations do not block the main thread, leading to smoother gameplay.

- **Job System**: CryEngine includes a job system that enables developers to create and manage tasks that can be executed on various threads. Jobs can be used to parallelize tasks like AI computations or resource loading.

```
// Example of creating and executing a job in CryEngine
JobSystem jobSystem;
JobHandle myJob = jobSystem.CreateJob();
jobSystem.RunJob(myJob, [](JobContext& context) {
    // Perform work in parallel
});
```

- **Rendering**: Rendering tasks, such as scene rendering and post-processing effects, are often executed on separate threads in CryEngine to maximize GPU utilization.

2.3.3. Benefits of Multithreading

Implementing multithreading in CryEngine offers several advantages:

- **Improved Performance**: Multithreading allows you to utilize multiple CPU cores efficiently, leading to better overall performance and frame rates.

- **Responsive Gameplay**: Offloading resource-intensive tasks, like physics and rendering, to separate threads ensures that the game remains responsive even during complex calculations.

- **Parallelism**: Tasks that can be executed independently can run in parallel, reducing the time needed to complete them.

2.3.4. Challenges of Multithreading

While multithreading can greatly enhance game performance, it also introduces challenges that need to be addressed:

- **Synchronization**: Managing shared resources and ensuring that multiple threads do not access them simultaneously is a critical aspect of multithreading. Proper synchronization mechanisms, such as mutexes and semaphores, are essential.

- **Race Conditions**: Race conditions can occur when multiple threads access and modify shared data simultaneously, leading to unpredictable behavior. Careful programming and synchronization can help prevent race conditions.

- **Debugging**: Debugging multithreaded applications can be complex, as issues may not always be reproducible. CryEngine provides debugging tools to help identify and resolve multithreading-related problems.

- **Load Balancing**: Distributing tasks evenly across threads to avoid CPU core imbalances is essential for optimal multithreading performance.

2.3.5. Multithreading Best Practices

To make the most of multithreading in CryEngine, consider the following best practices:

- **Profile and Optimize**: Use profiling tools to identify performance bottlenecks and determine which tasks can benefit from multithreading. Focus on optimizing the most critical sections of your code.

- **Proper Synchronization**: Use synchronization primitives like mutexes and semaphores to protect shared resources and avoid data races.

- **Load Balancing**: Monitor CPU core usage and ensure that tasks are evenly distributed across available cores for balanced multithreading.

- **Error Handling**: Implement robust error handling for multithreaded code to gracefully handle exceptions and avoid crashes.

- **Testing**: Thoroughly test your multithreaded code to catch potential issues early in development.

In summary, multithreading and concurrent processing are essential techniques in CryEngine for improving game performance and responsiveness. By understanding CryEngine's multithreading model, addressing challenges, and following best practices, developers can harness the power of modern CPUs and create more immersive and performant games.

2.4. Advanced Debugging and Profiling Techniques

Effective debugging and profiling are essential aspects of game development, allowing developers to identify and address performance bottlenecks, bugs, and other issues. In CryEngine, a range of advanced debugging and profiling tools are available to help developers optimize their games and ensure they run smoothly. This section explores some of these techniques and tools.

2.4.1. CryEngine Profiler

The CryEngine Profiler is a powerful tool for analyzing the performance of your game. It provides detailed insights into various aspects of your game, including CPU and GPU usage, memory usage, and more. Developers can use the profiler to identify performance bottlenecks, frame rate issues, and memory leaks.

To enable the profiler, you can use CryEngine's profiling system:

```
// Enable the CryEngine Profiler
ProfilingSystem profilingSystem;
profilingSystem.EnableProfiler();
```

2.4.2. Real-Time Debugging

CryEngine offers real-time debugging features, allowing developers to inspect and modify game variables, pause execution, and step through code during runtime. This is particularly useful for tracking down and fixing bugs as they occur.

```
// Example of setting a breakpoint in CryEngine's debugger
DebuggingSystem debuggingSystem;
debuggingSystem.SetBreakpoint("MyFunction.cpp", 42);
```

2.4.3. Memory Debugging

Memory-related issues can be challenging to diagnose but are critical for game stability. CryEngine provides memory debugging tools to detect memory leaks and analyze memory usage. By enabling memory tracking and profiling, developers can identify areas where memory is allocated and deallocated, helping to prevent memory-related problems.

```
// Enable memory tracking and profiling in CryEngine
ProfilingSystem profilingSystem;
profilingSystem.EnableMemoryTracking();
```

2.4.4. Asset Inspection

CryEngine allows developers to inspect assets in real-time, making it easier to identify and diagnose issues with textures, models, animations, and other game assets. Asset inspection tools can display asset properties and help verify that assets are correctly imported and configured.

```
// Inspect a game asset in CryEngine
AssetInspector assetInspector;
assetInspector.InspectAsset("my_model.fbx");
```

2.4.5. Remote Debugging

CryEngine supports remote debugging, allowing developers to debug their games on remote machines or consoles. This is particularly useful for testing and optimizing games on different platforms.

```
// Enable remote debugging in CryEngine
DebuggingSystem debuggingSystem;
debuggingSystem.EnableRemoteDebugging("192.168.0.100", 1234);
```

2.4.6. Profiling Custom Code

Developers can use CryEngine's profiling API to profile custom code and gather performance data. This is invaluable for identifying bottlenecks within specific game systems or subsystems.

```
// Profiling custom code in CryEngine
ProfilingSystem profilingSystem;
ProfilingContext context = profilingSystem.CreateContext("MySubsystem");
profilingSystem.BeginContext(context);
// Code to profile
profilingSystem.EndContext(context);
```

2.4.7. Automated Testing

CryEngine supports automated testing, allowing developers to create test cases and run them automatically to verify the correctness and stability of their games. Automated tests help catch regressions and ensure that new code changes do not introduce bugs.

```
// Creating an automated test in CryEngine
AutomatedTestingSystem automatedTestingSystem;
automatedTestingSystem.CreateTest("MyGameTest");
automatedTestingSystem.RunTests();
```

2.4.8. Crash Dump Analysis

When a game crashes, CryEngine generates crash dump files that can be analyzed to pinpoint the cause of the crash. Developers can use tools to examine these dump files and diagnose issues, making it easier to fix crashes and improve game stability.

In conclusion, advanced debugging and profiling techniques are indispensable for game development in CryEngine. Whether you're using the profiler, real-time debugging, memory tracking, asset inspection, remote debugging, or custom profiling, these tools empower developers to optimize game performance, identify and fix bugs, and deliver a more stable and enjoyable gaming experience to players.

2.5. Code Optimization and Scalability

Code optimization is a crucial aspect of game development in CryEngine, aiming to improve performance and scalability while maintaining code readability and maintainability. In this section, we will explore various code optimization techniques and practices that can help you achieve better performance in your CryEngine projects.

2.5.1. Profiling and Benchmarking

Before optimizing your code, it's essential to identify performance bottlenecks accurately. CryEngine provides profiling tools that allow you to measure the performance of different parts of your game. Profiling helps you determine which sections of code are consuming the most resources and need optimization.

```
// Profiling code for performance analysis
ProfilingSystem profilingSystem;
profilingSystem.EnableProfiling();
```

In addition to profiling, benchmarking is another valuable technique. You can create benchmark tests to measure the execution time of specific code segments, helping you understand the impact of optimizations.

```
// Creating a benchmark test in CryEngine
BenchmarkSystem benchmarkSystem;
benchmarkSystem.CreateBenchmark("MyBenchmark");
benchmarkSystem.RunBenchmark("MyBenchmark");
```

2.5.2. Algorithmic Complexity

Choosing the right algorithms and data structures is crucial for optimizing code. Analyze the algorithmic complexity of your code to ensure that it scales well as the input size grows. Prefer algorithms with lower time complexity (e.g., $O(n)$ instead of $O(n^2)$) for processing large datasets.

2.5.3. Avoid Premature Optimization

Premature optimization, optimizing code before identifying performance bottlenecks, can lead to unnecessary complexity and reduced code maintainability. Focus on optimizing critical sections of your code that have a significant impact on performance and scalability.

2.5.4. Parallelization

Leverage multithreading and parallel processing to take advantage of multi-core CPUs. Divide computationally intensive tasks into smaller parallelizable units and distribute them across multiple threads to improve performance. CryEngine's job system can help facilitate parallelization.

```
// Utilizing CryEngine's job system for parallel processing
JobSystem jobSystem;
JobHandle myJob = jobSystem.CreateJob();
jobSystem.RunJob(myJob, [](JobContext& context) {
    // Perform work in parallel
});
```

2.5.5. Data-Oriented Design (DOD)

Adopt a data-oriented design approach to improve memory locality and cache efficiency. Organize data structures and access patterns to minimize cache misses and maximize data throughput. This can significantly impact the performance of systems like physics simulations and rendering.

2.5.6. SIMD (Single Instruction, Multiple Data)

Utilize SIMD instructions to perform parallel operations on data. CryEngine supports SIMD optimizations, allowing you to take advantage of these hardware capabilities to accelerate certain calculations, such as vector math.

```
// Example of SIMD optimization in CryEngine
#include <Cry_SIMD.h>
```

```cpp
__m128 vector1 = _mm_set_ps(1.0f, 2.0f, 3.0f, 4.0f);
__m128 vector2 = _mm_set_ps(4.0f, 3.0f, 2.0f, 1.0f);
__m128 result = _mm_add_ps(vector1, vector2);
```

2.5.7. Resource Management

Efficiently manage game resources like textures, models, and audio assets. Use resource streaming and on-demand loading to minimize memory usage. Unload resources that are no longer needed to free up resources for other parts of your game.

```cpp
// Resource management in CryEngine
ResourceSystem resourceSystem;
resourceSystem.LoadResource("my_texture.dds");
resourceSystem.UnloadResource("my_texture.dds");
```

2.5.8. Continuous Optimization

Code optimization is an ongoing process. Continuously monitor and optimize your code as your project evolves. Regularly reevaluate your performance goals and apply optimizations as needed to maintain a high level of performance and scalability.

2.5.9. Scalability Options

CryEngine provides scalability settings that allow players to adjust graphical and performance settings according to their hardware capabilities. Implement scalability options in your game to cater to a broader audience and ensure a smooth gaming experience on a variety of systems.

```cpp
// Implementing scalability settings in CryEngine
ScalabilitySystem scalabilitySystem;
scalabilitySystem.AddScalabilityGroup("GraphicsQuality", 0, 2);
scalabilitySystem.AddScalabilitySetting("Low", "GraphicsQuality", 0);
scalabilitySystem.AddScalabilitySetting("Medium", "GraphicsQuality", 1);
scalabilitySystem.AddScalabilitySetting("High", "GraphicsQuality", 2);
```

In conclusion, code optimization and scalability are essential considerations in CryEngine game development. By profiling, choosing efficient algorithms, embracing parallelization, adopting data-oriented design, leveraging SIMD instructions, and implementing resource management and scalability options, you can create high-performance games that provide a smooth gaming experience for players on a variety of hardware configurations.

Chapter 3: Expert Level Design and World Building

3.1. Complex Level Architectures and Layouts

Creating captivating and immersive game worlds is a central aspect of game development in CryEngine. Level design involves crafting environments that not only look visually appealing but also provide engaging gameplay experiences. In this section, we will delve into the art and science of designing complex level architectures and layouts in CryEngine.

3.1.1. Concept and Vision

Before diving into level design, it's crucial to establish a clear concept and vision for your game's environment. Define the narrative, theme, and mood you want to convey through your level. This vision will serve as a guiding principle throughout the design process.

3.1.2. Layout Planning

Planning the layout of your level is a critical initial step. Consider the flow of gameplay, player navigation, and the distribution of key elements such as objectives, enemies, and resources. Sketch out the level's overall structure, including the placement of rooms, corridors, and open spaces.

3.1.3. Modular Design

Modular design is a common approach in CryEngine level design. Create reusable building blocks or modules that can be assembled to construct various parts of your level. This approach streamlines level creation, encourages consistency, and allows for easy modifications.

```
// Example of modular design using prefabs in CryEngine
PrefabSystem prefabSystem;
PrefabModule wallModule = prefabSystem.CreateModule("Wall");
PrefabModule doorModule = prefabSystem.CreateModule("Door");
PrefabModule windowModule = prefabSystem.CreateModule("Window");

// Assemble modules to create level architecture
LevelArchitecture architecture;
architecture.AddModule(wallModule, 0, 0, 0);
architecture.AddModule(doorModule, 5, 0, 0);
architecture.AddModule(windowModule, 10, 0, 0);
```

3.1.4. Environmental Storytelling

Environmental storytelling is a technique that conveys narrative elements through the level's environment. Use props, decorations, and environmental details to tell a story, provide context, and immerse players in the game world. Pay attention to the placement of objects and their significance within the narrative.

3.1.5. Player Flow and Pacing

Player flow and pacing are critical considerations in level design. Create a balance between moments of action, exploration, and narrative progression. Guide players through the level using visual cues, lighting, and level architecture to maintain engagement.

3.1.6. Playtesting and Iteration

Playtesting is an iterative process that involves testing your level with real players to gather feedback and make improvements. Pay attention to player feedback on level difficulty, clarity, and overall experience. Iteratively refine your level based on this feedback.

```
// Conducting playtesting sessions and gathering feedback
PlaytestingSystem playtestingSystem;
playtestingSystem.StartSession();
// Players explore and provide feedback
playtestingSystem.EndSession();
```

3.1.7. Performance Optimization

Optimizing level performance is crucial to ensure smooth gameplay. Use CryEngine's profiling tools to identify performance bottlenecks within your level. Consider techniques like level streaming to dynamically load and unload parts of the level to conserve resources.

```
// Level streaming in CryEngine for performance optimization
LevelStreamingSystem streamingSystem;
streamingSystem.LoadLevel("Level1");
streamingSystem.UnloadLevel("Level2");
```

3.1.8. Lighting and Atmosphere

Lighting and atmosphere play a significant role in level design. Experiment with different lighting setups, shadows, and atmospheric effects to create the desired mood and ambiance. CryEngine provides advanced lighting tools to achieve stunning visuals.

```
// Configuring dynamic lighting in CryEngine
LightingSystem lightingSystem;
lightingSystem.SetAmbientLightColor(Color(0.2, 0.2, 0.2));
lightingSystem.CreateDirectionalLight(Vector3(0, -1, 0), Color(1, 1, 1));
```

3.1.9. Testing and QA

Thoroughly test your level for bugs, glitches, and unintended player interactions. Engage quality assurance (QA) testers to identify and report issues. Conduct regression testing to ensure that changes to your level do not introduce new problems.

3.1.10. Documentation

Documentation is essential for communicating level design concepts and guidelines to your team. Create clear and concise documentation that outlines the level's objectives, layout, asset usage, and any specific design considerations.

In conclusion, complex level architecture and layout design are essential components of creating memorable and engaging game environments in CryEngine. By defining a clear vision, planning the layout, using modular design, incorporating environmental storytelling, optimizing performance, and considering lighting and atmosphere, you can craft levels that captivate players and enhance the overall gaming experience. Playtesting, iteration, and effective documentation are key to refining your level design and delivering a polished product to players.

3.2. Dynamic World Building Techniques

Dynamic world building is an integral part of level design in CryEngine, allowing for interactive and ever-evolving game environments. In this section, we will explore various techniques and tools for creating dynamic worlds that respond to player actions and enhance immersion.

3.2.1. Procedural Generation

Procedural generation is a powerful technique that can be used to create dynamic landscapes, terrain, and assets within your game world. CryEngine provides tools and scripting support to implement procedural generation, enabling the creation of vast and diverse game worlds.

```
// Example of procedural terrain generation in CryEngine
TerrainSystem terrainSystem;
terrainSystem.GenerateProceduralTerrain(512, 512);
```

3.2.2. Interactive Elements

Incorporate interactive elements into your game world to engage players and enhance immersion. Objects that can be moved, triggered, or manipulated provide opportunities for puzzle-solving, exploration, and dynamic storytelling.

```
// Creating an interactive lever in CryEngine
InteractiveObject lever;
lever.Initialize("Lever", Vector3(10, 0, 5));
lever.OnInteract([](Player& player) {
    // Perform interactive action
});
```

3.2.3. Dynamic Events and Triggers

Implement dynamic events and triggers that respond to player actions. These events can include scripted sequences, environmental changes, or enemy encounters triggered by the player's progression or decisions.

```
// Defining a dynamic event triggered by player proximity
DynamicEvent event;
event.SetTrigger(Trigger::Proximity);
event.OnTrigger([]() {
    // Execute dynamic event
});
```

3.2.4. Weather and Time of Day

Dynamic weather and time-of-day systems can significantly impact the atmosphere of your game world. Create changing weather patterns, day-night cycles, and seasonal variations to add realism and variety to your levels.

```
// Implementing a dynamic time-of-day system in CryEngine
TimeOfDaySystem timeOfDaySystem;
timeOfDaySystem.SetTime(12, 0);
timeOfDaySystem.AdvanceTime(1); // Advance one hour
```

3.2.5. Environmental Destruction

Introduce environmental destruction to your game world to create dynamic and immersive combat experiences. CryEngine supports destructible objects and terrain, allowing for realistic destruction physics.

```
// Enabling environmental destruction in CryEngine
DestructionSystem destructionSystem;
destructionSystem.EnableDestruction();
```

3.2.6. Randomization

Randomization is a useful technique for introducing variability and unpredictability into your game world. Use randomization to spawn enemies, loot, and environmental elements in different locations or with varying attributes.

```
// Randomly spawning enemies in CryEngine
EnemySpawner enemySpawner;
enemySpawner.SpawnRandomEnemy();
```

3.2.7. Player Choices and Consequences

Implement branching narratives and player choices that affect the game world. Allow players to make decisions that influence the storyline, character relationships, and the state of the game world.

```
// Managing player choices and consequences in CryEngine
ChoiceSystem choiceSystem;
```

```
choiceSystem.AddChoice("Save the villagers", []() {
    // Outcome based on player choice
});
choiceSystem.AddChoice("Abandon the quest", []() {
    // Different outcome based on player choice
});
```

3.2.8. Dynamic AI Behavior

Create dynamic AI behavior that adapts to changing circumstances. Use behavior trees, decision-making algorithms, and sensory systems to make AI characters respond realistically to the player's actions and the state of the world.

```
// Implementing dynamic AI behavior in CryEngine
AISystem aiSystem;
AICharacter enemy;
enemy.SetBehaviorTree("AggressiveBehavior");
```

3.2.9. Performance Considerations

While dynamic world building adds depth to your game, it can also be resource-intensive. Ensure that your dynamic systems are optimized to maintain smooth gameplay. Use level streaming, resource management, and LOD (Level of Detail) techniques to balance performance and dynamism.

3.2.10. Playtesting and Iteration

Dynamic world building requires thorough playtesting to identify and resolve issues related to player interactions, event triggers, and system responsiveness. Iteratively refine your dynamic systems based on player feedback and testing results.

In conclusion, dynamic world building techniques in CryEngine open up exciting possibilities for creating immersive and ever-evolving game environments. By incorporating procedural generation, interactive elements, dynamic events, weather and time systems, environmental destruction, randomization, player choices, dynamic AI behavior, and considering performance, you can craft dynamic game worlds that captivate players and offer rich and engaging experiences. Playtesting and iteration are essential to fine-tune your dynamic systems and deliver a polished gameplay experience.

3.3. Creating Immersive and Interactive Environments

Creating immersive and interactive environments is a core aspect of level design in CryEngine. Immersion involves making players feel like they are part of the game world, while interactivity encourages engagement and exploration. In this section, we will explore techniques and practices to achieve both these goals in your CryEngine levels.

3.3.1. Environmental Detail

Pay attention to environmental detail to create a sense of realism and immersion. Use textures, props, and decorations to add richness to your game world. Consider factors like weathering, wear and tear, and environmental storytelling to make the environment feel lived-in.

```
// Adding environmental details in CryEngine
EnvironmentalDetailSystem detailSystem;
detailSystem.AddFoliage("Grass", Vector3(20, 0, 10));
detailSystem.AddDecal("BulletHoles", Vector3(15, 2, 8));
```

3.3.2. Audio Design

Sound design plays a crucial role in creating an immersive environment. Utilize CryEngine's audio tools to add ambient sounds, music, and sound effects that complement the visual experience. Consider spatial audio to enhance the sense of location and directionality.

```
// Implementing audio design in CryEngine
AudioSystem audioSystem;
audioSystem.PlaySound("ForestAmbience", Vector3(0, 0, 0));
audioSystem.PlayMusic("ExplorationTheme");
```

3.3.3. Lighting and Atmosphere

Lighting and atmospheric effects are key to creating immersive environments. Experiment with different lighting setups, use dynamic shadows, and employ post-processing effects to achieve the desired mood and atmosphere in your levels.

```
// Configuring atmospheric lighting in CryEngine
LightingSystem lightingSystem;
lightingSystem.SetAmbientLightColor(Color(0.2, 0.2, 0.2));
lightingSystem.CreateDirectionalLight(Vector3(0, -1, 0), Color(1, 1, 1));
```

3.3.4. Environmental Interaction

Make the environment interactive by allowing players to interact with objects and elements in meaningful ways. Enable physics interactions, such as moving objects, pushing buttons, or solving puzzles, to engage players and provide a sense of agency.

```
// Enabling environmental interaction in CryEngine
InteractiveObject lever;
lever.Initialize("Lever", Vector3(10, 0, 5));
lever.OnInteract([](Player& player) {
    // Perform interactive action
});
```

3.3.5. Environmental Hazards

Incorporate environmental hazards that pose challenges to players. Hazards like traps, collapsing structures, and natural disasters add excitement and require players to react quickly, enhancing the level's interactivity.

```
// Creating environmental hazards in CryEngine
EnvironmentalHazard trap;
trap.Initialize("Spikes", Vector3(8, 0, 12));
trap.OnTrigger([](Player& player) {
    // Apply damage or perform hazard-specific actions
});
```

3.3.6. Non-Player Characters (NPCs)

Introduce non-player characters (NPCs) into your environment to make it feel alive. NPCs can provide information, quests, or even serve as enemies. Implement AI behaviors that allow NPCs to interact with the player and the world.

```
// Adding non-player characters in CryEngine
AISystem aiSystem;
AICharacter npc;
npc.Initialize("Merchant", Vector3(5, 0, 3));
npc.SetBehaviorTree("MerchantBehavior");
```

3.3.7. Storytelling Elements

Integrate storytelling elements into your environment. Use environmental clues, notes, journals, and visual storytelling to convey the game's narrative and lore. Engage players in uncovering the story as they explore the environment.

```
// Implementing storytelling elements in CryEngine
StorytellingSystem storytellingSystem;
storytellingSystem.AddJournal("Explorer's Notes", Vector3(12, 1, 7));
storytellingSystem.AddClue("Mysterious Symbol", Vector3(18, 2, 14));
```

3.3.8. Accessibility

Consider accessibility in your level design. Ensure that interactive elements and storytelling are accessible to players with different abilities. Provide options for adjusting the difficulty level to accommodate a wide range of players.

3.3.9. Playtesting and Feedback

Playtesting is essential to evaluate the effectiveness of your immersive and interactive elements. Gather feedback from players to identify areas where immersion can be improved and interactivity enhanced. Iterate on your design based on player input.

3.3.10. Performance Optimization

While creating immersive environments, be mindful of performance. Use CryEngine's profiling tools to ensure that the additional detail, audio, and interactivity do not negatively impact the game's performance. Employ level streaming and LOD techniques to manage resource usage.

In conclusion, creating immersive and interactive environments in CryEngine requires careful consideration of environmental detail, audio design, lighting, interactivity, environmental hazards, NPCs, storytelling, accessibility, playtesting, and performance optimization. By combining these elements, you can craft game worlds that captivate players, draw them into the experience, and provide a sense of immersion and agency within the environment.

3.4. Advanced Lighting and Atmospheric Effects

Advanced lighting and atmospheric effects are essential components of level design in CryEngine, contributing to the visual quality and mood of the game environment. In this section, we will explore techniques and practices for implementing sophisticated lighting and atmospheric effects in your CryEngine levels.

3.4.1. Global Illumination (GI)

Global Illumination is a rendering technique that simulates indirect lighting, improving the realism of scenes. CryEngine supports various GI methods, including voxel-based, radiosity, and ray tracing. Choose the method that best suits your project's requirements.

```
// Enabling global illumination in CryEngine
RenderingSystem renderingSystem;
renderingSystem.EnableGlobalIllumination(true);
```

3.4.2. Real-Time Reflections

Real-time reflections enhance the visual quality of game environments by reflecting dynamic objects and scenery in reflective surfaces. CryEngine's reflection probes and screen space reflections provide solutions for implementing real-time reflections.

```
// Implementing real-time reflections in CryEngine
ReflectionSystem reflectionSystem;
reflectionSystem.EnableReflectionProbes(true);
reflectionSystem.EnableScreenSpaceReflections(true);
```

3.4.3. Dynamic Day-Night Cycles

Dynamic day-night cycles create immersive environments with changing lighting conditions. Use CryEngine's time-of-day system to control the sun's position, atmospheric scattering, and the color of the sky and lighting to achieve realistic day-night transitions.

```
// Configuring dynamic day-night cycles in CryEngine
TimeOfDaySystem timeOfDaySystem;
timeOfDaySystem.SetTime(12, 0);
timeOfDaySystem.AdvanceTime(1); // Advance one hour
```

3.4.4. Weather Effects

Implement weather effects such as rain, snow, fog, and wind to add variety and atmosphere to your levels. CryEngine provides tools for simulating and rendering weather effects realistically.

```
// Adding weather effects in CryEngine
WeatherSystem weatherSystem;
weatherSystem.SetWeather(Weather::Rain);
```

3.4.5. Particle Systems

Particle systems are valuable for creating atmospheric effects like smoke, fire, dust, and sparks. CryEngine's particle editor allows you to design and customize particle effects to suit your level's atmosphere.

```
// Configuring a particle system for smoke in CryEngine
ParticleSystem smokeSystem;
ParticleEmitter smokeEmitter;
smokeEmitter.SetTexture("SmokeParticleTexture");
smokeEmitter.SetColor(Color(0.7, 0.7, 0.7));
```

3.4.6. Post-Processing Effects

Post-processing effects, such as depth of field, bloom, and color grading, can dramatically enhance the visual appeal of your levels. Experiment with various post-processing settings to achieve the desired cinematic look.

```
// Applying post-processing effects in CryEngine
PostProcessingSystem postProcessingSystem;
postProcessingSystem.EnableDepthOfField(true);
postProcessingSystem.SetBloomIntensity(0.5);
postProcessingSystem.ApplyColorGrading("CinematicLook");
```

3.4.7. Light Probes and Baking

Light probes and light baking techniques help optimize lighting in your levels. Use light probes to capture and interpolate lighting information, reducing runtime calculations. Baking static lighting can improve performance while maintaining high-quality visuals.

```
// Implementing light probes and baking in CryEngine
LightingSystem lightingSystem;
lightingSystem.EnableLightProbes(true);
lightingSystem.EnableLightBaking(true);
```

3.4.8. Shadow Mapping

Shadow mapping techniques enable realistic shadows in your levels. CryEngine supports cascaded shadow maps and dynamic shadow resolution adjustment to provide high-quality, performance-efficient shadows.

```
// Configuring shadow mapping in CryEngine
ShadowMappingSystem shadowMappingSystem;
shadowMappingSystem.EnableCascadedShadowMaps(true);
shadowMappingSystem.AdjustShadowResolution(true);
```

3.4.9. Performance Optimization

While advanced lighting and atmospheric effects can enhance visuals, they may also impact performance. Use CryEngine's profiling tools to identify performance bottlenecks related to rendering. Adjust settings, such as GI quality and shadow map resolution, to balance visual fidelity and performance.

3.4.10. Cross-Platform Considerations

Consider the capabilities of different target platforms when implementing advanced lighting and atmospheric effects. Optimize settings and effects for various hardware configurations to ensure a consistent experience for players.

In conclusion, advanced lighting and atmospheric effects are vital for creating visually stunning and immersive game environments in CryEngine. By leveraging global illumination, real-time reflections, dynamic day-night cycles, weather effects, particle systems, post-processing effects, light probes, shadow mapping, and optimizing for performance and cross-platform compatibility, you can craft levels that captivate players with their visual quality and atmosphere. Balancing these effects with performance considerations is key to delivering an enjoyable and visually appealing gaming experience.

3.5. Integrating Storytelling Elements into Level Design

Integrating storytelling elements into level design is a fundamental aspect of creating engaging and immersive game experiences in CryEngine. In this section, we will explore various techniques and strategies for seamlessly weaving narrative elements into your levels.

3.5.1. Environmental Storytelling

Environmental storytelling involves using the game environment itself to convey narrative elements. Place objects, props, and visual cues strategically within your level to provide context, backstory, and hints about the game world and its history.

```
// Placing environmental storytelling elements in CryEngine
StorytellingSystem storytellingSystem;
storytellingSystem.AddNote("Journal Entry", Vector3(15, 1, 10));
storytellingSystem.AddMysteriousSymbol(Vector3(12, 2, 8));
```

3.5.2. Non-Player Characters (NPCs)

Incorporate non-player characters (NPCs) into your levels to interact with the player and deliver narrative information. NPCs can serve as quest givers, allies, or antagonists, enriching the storyline and providing depth to the game world.

```
// Adding non-player characters in CryEngine
AISystem aiSystem;
AICharacter npc;
npc.Initialize("QuestGiver", Vector3(5, 0, 3));
npc.SetDialogue("QuestDialogue");
```

3.5.3. Dialogue and Voice Over

Implement dialogue systems that allow characters to communicate with the player. Use voice-over recordings, text-based dialogue trees, or a combination of both to convey conversations and progress the narrative.

```
// Implementing dialogue with voice over in CryEngine
DialogSystem dialogSystem;
dialogSystem.StartConversation("CharacterA", "Hello, adventurer.");
dialogSystem.AddOption("Ask about the quest", [](){
    // NPC responds with quest details
});
dialogSystem.AddOption("Leave", [](){
    // End conversation
});
```

3.5.4. Quests and Objectives

Integrate quests, objectives, and tasks into your levels to drive the narrative forward. Create a clear and engaging quest structure that encourages player exploration and interaction with the game world.

```
// Designing quests and objectives in CryEngine
QuestSystem questSystem;
questSystem.AddQuest("Retrieve the Lost Artifact");
questSystem.AddObjective("Find the artifact in the crypt");
questSystem.AddObjective("Return the artifact to the quest giver");
```

3.5.5. Cutscenes and Cinematics

Craft cinematic moments and cutscenes to deliver important story beats. CryEngine's cinematic tools allow you to create scripted sequences with camera angles, character animations, and visual effects.

```
// Creating a cinematic cutscene in CryEngine
CinematicSystem cinematicSystem;
cinematicSystem.PlayCutscene("IntroductionCutscene");
```

3.5.6. Interactive Storytelling

Engage players in interactive storytelling by allowing them to make choices that impact the narrative. Implement branching storylines and multiple endings based on player decisions, fostering player agency and immersion.

```
// Managing player choices and consequences in CryEngine
ChoiceSystem choiceSystem;
choiceSystem.AddChoice("Accept the quest", []() {
    // Quest progresses based on player choice
});
choiceSystem.AddChoice("Decline the quest", []() {
    // Different outcome based on player choice
});
```

3.5.7. Story-Driven Level Design

Design levels that are inherently tied to the game's narrative. Ensure that the environments players explore resonate with the story, whether it's a mysterious dungeon, a futuristic cityscape, or an enchanted forest.

```
// Designing a story-driven level in CryEngine
LevelDesignSystem levelDesignSystem;
levelDesignSystem.CreateDungeonLevel("Crypt of Legends");
```

3.5.8. Clues and Mysteries

Incorporate clues and mysteries within your levels to encourage players to investigate and uncover hidden secrets. These elements can add depth to the narrative and reward players for their curiosity.

```
// Adding clues and mysteries in CryEngine
StorytellingSystem storytellingSystem;
storytellingSystem.AddClue("Mysterious Map", Vector3(18, 2, 14));
storytellingSystem.AddMysteriousStatue(Vector3(20, 0, 10));
```

3.5.9. Player Engagement and Feedback

Gather player feedback to assess the effectiveness of your storytelling elements. Ensure that the narrative is engaging, coherent, and emotionally resonant. Iterate on your level design based on player input to enhance the storytelling experience.

3.5.10. Accessibility and Inclusivity

Consider accessibility in your storytelling. Ensure that narrative elements are presented in a way that accommodates players with different abilities. Provide subtitles, text-to-speech options, and adjustable difficulty settings for a broader audience.

In conclusion, integrating storytelling elements into level design in CryEngine is a multifaceted process that involves environmental storytelling, NPCs, dialogue, quests, cutscenes, interactive storytelling, story-driven level design, clues, and player engagement. By skillfully weaving these elements into your levels, you can create a narrative-rich gaming experience that captivates players, immerses them in the game world, and keeps them engaged in the unfolding story. Continuously gathering player feedback and ensuring accessibility further enhance the storytelling aspect of your CryEngine game.

Chapter 4: Realistic Character and Creature Creation

4.1. High-Fidelity Character Modeling

High-fidelity character modeling is a crucial aspect of game development in CryEngine, as it directly impacts the visual quality and realism of characters and creatures within your game world. In this section, we will explore the techniques and best practices for creating detailed and lifelike character models that seamlessly integrate into CryEngine-powered games.

4.1.1. Character Concept and Design

Before diving into character modeling, it's essential to have a clear character concept and design in place. Define the character's appearance, personality, backstory, and role within the game's narrative. This concept will serve as a guiding blueprint for your modeling efforts.

4.1.2. Reference Gathering

Gather visual references and inspiration for your character model. Collect images, sketches, and concept art that align with your character's design. Reference materials will help you achieve accuracy and realism in your modeling work.

4.1.3. Choosing Modeling Software

Select a 3D modeling software that you are comfortable with and that supports CryEngine's asset import requirements. Popular choices include Blender, Autodesk Maya, and 3ds Max. Familiarize yourself with the modeling tool's features and capabilities.

4.1.4. Character Topology

Pay close attention to the topology of your character model. Ensure that the mesh is well-structured with clean edge loops and efficient geometry. Proper topology is essential for smooth deformations during animation.

```
// Example of character mesh topology in 3D modeling software
CharacterModel character;
character.SetTopology("CleanTopology.fbx");
```

4.1.5. High-Resolution Sculpting

Use high-resolution sculpting tools like ZBrush or Mudbox to add intricate details to your character. Sculpt fine wrinkles, skin pores, muscle definition, and other fine features to enhance realism.

```
// High-resolution sculpting for character details
CharacterModel character;
character.SculptDetails("Wrinkles", "SkinPores", "MuscleDefinition");
```

4.1.6. UV Mapping

Create efficient UV maps for your character model to ensure proper texture placement and mapping. Well-organized UV layouts make it easier to apply textures and materials later.

```
// UV mapping for character model
CharacterModel character;
character.GenerateUVMap("CharacterUVs");
```

4.1.7. Texturing and Material Assignments

Apply high-quality textures and materials to your character model to bring it to life. Utilize texture maps for diffuse, specular, normal, and other material properties. CryEngine supports PBR (Physically Based Rendering), so ensure that your textures adhere to PBR principles.

```
// Texturing and material assignment for character
CharacterModel character;
character.ApplyTexture("Character_Diffuse", "Character_Normal", "Character_Sp
ecular");
```

4.1.8. Rigging and Skinning

Rig your character model with a skeletal structure and weight painting. This allows for realistic animations and deformations. CryEngine supports various animation formats, so ensure compatibility.

```
// Rigging and skinning for character animation
CharacterModel character;
character.ApplySkeleton("CharacterSkeleton");
character.SetWeightPainting("SkinWeights");
```

4.1.9. Animation Integration

Integrate animations into CryEngine for your character model. Create or import animations for idle, walking, running, combat, and other character actions. Test and refine animations to ensure they align with the character's design and role.

```
// Integrating character animations in CryEngine
AnimationSystem animationSystem;
animationSystem.ImportAnimations("CharacterAnimations.fbx");
```

4.1.10. Optimization and LODs

Optimize your character model for runtime performance. Implement Level of Detail (LOD) models to ensure that characters retain visual quality while reducing polygon count at a distance.

```
// Implementing LODs for character models in CryEngine
CharacterModel character;
character.CreateLODs("LOD0", "LOD1", "LOD2");
```

4.1.11. Testing and Iteration

Thoroughly test your character model within CryEngine. Ensure that animations, materials, and textures work correctly in the game engine. Gather feedback from testers and iterate on your model to address any issues or improvements.

4.1.12. Export and Integration

Once your character model is finalized, export it in a compatible format for CryEngine (e.g., FBX) and integrate it into your game project. Ensure proper scaling, positioning, and asset organization.

```
// Exporting and integrating character model in CryEngine
CharacterModel character;
character.ExportAndIntegrate("CharacterModel.fbx");
```

In conclusion, high-fidelity character modeling in CryEngine is a multi-faceted process that involves character concept and design, reference gathering, choice of modeling software, topology, high-resolution sculpting, UV mapping, texturing and material assignments, rigging and skinning, animation integration,

---

4.2. Advanced Rigging and Animation Techniques

In the realm of game development with CryEngine, advanced rigging and animation techniques are essential for bringing characters and creatures to life. This section delves into the intricacies of rigging and animation, exploring the methods and practices that will help you create lifelike and dynamic character movements.

4.2.1. Rigging Fundamentals

Rigging involves creating a skeletal structure for your characters, enabling them to move and deform realistically. In CryEngine, you can use tools such as the CryEngine Mannequin Editor to set up rigs for characters. A well-structured rig ensures smooth and believable animations.

```
// Setting up a character rig in the CryEngine Mannequin Editor
CharacterRig characterRig;
characterRig.CreateSkeleton("CharacterSkeleton");
characterRig.AddIKConstraints("LeftArmIK", "RightLegIK");
```

4.2.2. Inverse Kinematics (IK)

Inverse Kinematics allows you to control specific parts of a character's body more precisely. Implementing IK for limbs, hands, or feet can improve animation quality, especially in scenarios where precise positioning is required.

```
// Implementing Inverse Kinematics for character limbs in CryEngine
CharacterRig characterRig;
characterRig.AddIKConstraints("LeftArmIK", "RightLegIK");
```

4.2.3. Facial Rigging

Facial rigging is crucial for conveying emotions and expressions in characters. Use CryEngine's facial rigging tools to create a system that allows characters to emote realistically.

```
// Setting up facial rigging for character expressions in CryEngine
CharacterRig characterRig;
characterRig.CreateFacialRig("FacialRig");
```

4.2.4. Blend Trees

Blend trees are essential for smoothly transitioning between animations and creating complex character movements. CryEngine supports blend trees, allowing you to blend animations based on various parameters like speed, direction, and more.

```
// Implementing blend trees for character animations in CryEngine
AnimationSystem animationSystem;
animationSystem.CreateBlendTree("MovementBlendTree");
```

4.2.5. Motion Capture Integration

Motion capture technology can significantly enhance the realism of character animations. Integrate motion capture data into CryEngine by importing and retargeting animations to your character's rig.

```
// Integrating motion capture data into CryEngine
AnimationSystem animationSystem;
animationSystem.ImportMotionCaptureData("MocapData.fbx");
```

4.2.6. Animation State Machines

Animation state machines allow you to define the logic governing character animations. Use CryEngine's animation state machine editor to create complex animation behaviors, such as transitioning between idle, walking, running, and combat states.

```
// Designing animation state machines in CryEngine
AnimationStateMachine animationStateMachine;
animationStateMachine.CreateState("IdleState");
animationStateMachine.CreateState("WalkState");
animationStateMachine.CreateTransition("IdleToWalk", "IdleState", "WalkState"
);
```

4.2.7. Layered Animations

Layered animations enable you to add secondary movements or details to characters. For example, you can layer breathing animations on top of walking animations to create a more natural look.

```
// Implementing layered animations in CryEngine
AnimationLayer animationLayer;
animationLayer.AddLayer("BreathingLayer");
animationLayer.SetWeight("BreathingLayer", 0.5);
```

4.2.8. Animation Blending and Crossfading

Smooth transitions between animations are critical for character believability. Use CryEngine's animation blending and crossfading techniques to achieve seamless transitions, whether it's blending between idle and walking or transitioning from one combat move to another.

```
// Implementing animation blending and crossfading in CryEngine
AnimationSystem animationSystem;
animationSystem.CrossfadeAnimations("Idle", "Walking", 0.2);
```

4.2.9. Physics-Based Animation

Incorporate physics-based animation to add realism to character movements. Physics-based systems can handle interactions like cloth simulation, hair physics, and ragdoll effects.

```
// Adding physics-based animation for character cloth simulation
PhysicsSystem physicsSystem;
physicsSystem.EnableClothSimulation("CharacterCloth");
```

4.2.10. Testing and Debugging

Thoroughly test animations in CryEngine to ensure they function as intended. Debug any issues related to rigging, animation states, or blending to create a polished and glitch-free character animation system.

4.2.11. Animation Optimization

Optimize animations for runtime performance. Consider implementing LODs for animations to reduce memory and processing requirements, especially for distant characters.

```
// Implementing LODs for character animations in CryEngine
AnimationSystem animationSystem;
animationSystem.CreateLODs("LOD0", "LOD1", "LOD2");
```

4.2.12. Export and Integration

Once animations are complete, export them in a compatible format (e.g., FBX) and integrate them into CryEngine. Ensure that animations align with the character's rig and are correctly set up in the game engine.

```
// Exporting and integrating character animations in CryEngine
CharacterModel character;
character.ExportAndIntegrate("CharacterAnimations.fbx");
```

In conclusion, advanced rigging and animation techniques play a pivotal role in creating characters and creatures that feel alive in CryEngine-powered games. These techniques encompass rigging fundamentals, inverse kinematics, facial rigging, blend trees, motion capture integration, animation state machines, layered animations, animation blending and crossfading, physics-based animation, testing and debugging, animation optimization, and export and integration. Mastering these techniques allows you to craft captivating and realistic character animations that enhance the overall gaming experience.

4.3. Creating Believable Creatures and Monsters

Creating believable creatures and monsters is a fascinating and integral part of game development in CryEngine. These unique entities add depth and challenge to a game world, immersing players in thrilling experiences. In this section, we will explore the art and science of designing and animating creatures and monsters that feel both believable and terrifying.

4.3.1. Creature Concept and Design

The process begins with a well-defined concept and design for your creature or monster. Determine its appearance, behavior, and role within the game. Consider its origins, abilities, weaknesses, and how it fits into the game's narrative.

4.3.2. Visual References

Gather visual references to inspire and guide your creature design. Study real-world animals, mythological creatures, and artistic interpretations to create a visually compelling and coherent creature.

```
// Collecting visual references for creature design
CreatureDesign creatureDesign;
creatureDesign.AddReferences("WildlifePhotos", "MythologicalArt", "ConceptSke
tches");
```

4.3.3. Anatomy and Physiology

Understand the anatomy and physiology of your creature. Consider its skeletal structure, muscle placement, and how it moves. Ensure that its design adheres to the principles of biomechanics.

```
// Analyzing creature anatomy for realistic design
CreatureModel creatureModel;
creatureModel.AnalyzeAnatomy("SkeletalStructure", "MusclePlacement");
```

4.3.4. Texture and Material Design

Create detailed textures and materials for your creature. Pay attention to skin, fur, scales, or any unique features that define its appearance. Utilize CryEngine's PBR materials to achieve realistic rendering.

```
// Designing creature textures and materials in CryEngine
CreatureModel creatureModel;
creatureModel.ApplyTexture("Creature_Skin", "Creature_Normal", "Creature_Spec
ular");
```

4.3.5. Rigging and Animation

Rig your creature model with a suitable skeletal structure. Consider the creature's size and movement capabilities when designing the rig. Develop animations that reflect its behavior, whether it's a lumbering giant or a swift predator.

```
// Rigging and animating a creature in CryEngine
CreatureModel creatureModel;
creatureModel.ApplySkeleton("CreatureSkeleton");
creatureModel.CreateAnimations("Walking", "Attacking", "Idle");
```

4.3.6. Unique Behaviors

Give your creature unique behaviors and abilities. Think about its interactions with the player and the game environment. Create compelling AI patterns that make encounters with the creature engaging and challenging.

```
// Implementing unique behaviors for a game creature
CreatureAI creatureAI;
creatureAI.DefineBehavior("AmbushPredator");
creatureAI.SetAttackPattern("SurpriseAttack");
creatureAI.SetWeakness("FireDamage");
```

4.3.7. Sound Design

Sound plays a vital role in creature believability. Design and implement distinct sounds for your creature, including growls, roars, footsteps, and other vocalizations. Use spatial audio to enhance immersion.

```
// Sound design for a game creature in CryEngine
CreatureSound creatureSound;
creatureSound.CreateVocalizations("Roar", "Growl", "Snarl");
creatureSound.AssignSpatialAudio("CreatureAudioZone");
```

4.3.8. AI Behavior Trees

Implement AI behavior trees to control the creature's actions and reactions. Define states such as idle, alert, pursue, and attack. Behavior trees provide a structured approach to AI decision-making.

```
// Creating an AI behavior tree for a game creature
CreatureAI creatureAI;
creatureAI.CreateBehaviorTree("CreatureBehaviorTree");
creatureAI.DefineStates("Idle", "Alert", "Pursue", "Attack");
```

4.3.9. Testing and Balancing

Thoroughly playtest encounters with your creature to ensure that its behavior is challenging but fair. Balance its abilities and weaknesses to provide a satisfying gameplay experience.

4.3.10. Environmental Integration

Consider how the creature interacts with the game environment. Implement pathfinding, collision detection, and destructible terrain where applicable. Ensure that the creature feels integrated into the world.

```
// Environmental integration for a game creature
CreatureAI creatureAI;
creatureAI.IntegratePathfinding("CreaturePathfinding");
creatureAI.HandleTerrainDestruction("DestructibleTerrain");
```

4.3.11. Variation and Mutations

Introduce variation among creatures of the same type. Consider mutations, color variations, or unique characteristics. This adds diversity to encounters and keeps players engaged.

```
// Adding variation and mutations to game creatures
CreatureModel creatureModel;
creatureModel.CreateVariations("AlphaVariant", "BetaVariant", "GammaVariant")
;
```

4.3.12. Narrative Integration

Integrate your creature into the game's narrative. Provide lore or backstory that explains its existence and role within the game world. This enhances immersion and player engagement.

In conclusion, creating believable creatures and monsters in CryEngine involves a comprehensive process that encompasses concept and design, visual references, anatomy and physiology, texture and material design, rigging and animation, unique behaviors, sound design, AI behavior trees, testing and balancing, environmental integration, variation and mutations, and narrative integration. These elements combine to bring your creatures to life, making them memorable and integral to the gaming experience.

4.4. Motion Capture Integration and Enhancement

Motion capture (mocap) technology has revolutionized character animation in the gaming industry, allowing for highly realistic and natural movements. In this section, we will explore the process of motion capture integration and enhancement in CryEngine, enabling you to bring lifelike animations to your characters and creatures.

4.4.1. Understanding Motion Capture

Motion capture involves recording the movements of real actors or objects and translating them into digital animations. This technology captures subtle nuances and details that are challenging to achieve with traditional animation techniques.

4.4.2. Choosing the Right Mocap System

Selecting the appropriate motion capture system is crucial. Consider factors like the number of cameras, markerless vs. marker-based systems, and the level of precision required for your game's animations.

```
// Choosing a motion capture system for your game project
MotionCaptureSystem mocapSystem;
mocapSystem.SelectSystem("HighPrecisionMarkerBased");
```

4.4.3. Setting Up Mocap Sessions

Plan and organize mocap sessions with actors or performers who will provide the motion data. Ensure that the capture environment is well-lit and calibrated for accurate results.

```
// Organizing mocap sessions for character animations
MotionCaptureSystem mocapSystem;
mocapSystem.SetUpSession("Actor1", "Actor2", "SessionDate");
```

4.4.4. Capturing Raw Data

During mocap sessions, record raw motion data, including body movements, facial expressions, and any relevant actions. High-quality mocap data is the foundation of realistic animations.

```
// Capturing raw motion data during mocap sessions
MotionCaptureSystem mocapSystem;
mocapSystem.CaptureRawData("FullBodyMocap", "FacialExpressions", "ActionSeque
nces");
```

4.4.5. Data Cleaning and Refinement

Raw mocap data often requires cleaning and refinement to remove noise and errors. Use motion capture software to process and enhance the captured animations.

```
// Cleaning and refining mocap data for smoother animations
MotionCaptureTools mocapTools;
mocapTools.CleanData("RemoveNoise", "FixJitter", "SmoothTransitions");
```

4.4.6. Rigging and Retargeting

Integrate the cleaned mocap data into your character rigs. Ensure that the skeleton structure of the character matches the mocap data. Retargeting tools help map the actor's movements to the character's rig.

```
// Rigging and retargeting mocap data for character animations
CharacterRig characterRig;
characterRig.ApplyMocapData("MocapSkeleton", "RetargetingSettings");
```

4.4.7. Combining Mocap and Keyframe Animations

In many cases, a game may use a combination of mocap and keyframe animations. Blend or combine these animations seamlessly to achieve the desired character movements.

```
// Blending mocap and keyframe animations for character actions
AnimationSystem animationSystem;
animationSystem.BlendAnimations("MocapWalk", "KeyframeIdle", "TransitionTime"
);
```

4.4.8. Facial Mocap Integration

Facial mocap is essential for realistic character expressions and lip syncing. Integrate facial mocap data into your character's facial rig to synchronize facial animations with dialogues.

```
// Integrating facial mocap data for character lip syncing
CharacterFacialRig facialRig;
facialRig.ApplyFacialMocap("LipSyncData", "ExpressionMapping");
```

4.4.9. Testing and Iteration

Thoroughly test and iterate on mocap-integrated animations within CryEngine. Ensure that character movements, facial expressions, and lip syncing align with the game's requirements.

4.4.10. Optimization and Compression

Optimize mocap data for runtime performance. Use compression techniques to reduce memory usage while maintaining animation quality.

```
// Optimizing mocap data for efficient runtime performance
AnimationSystem animationSystem;
animationSystem.CompressAnimations("MocapAnimations", "CompressionSettings");
```

4.4.11. Environmental Interaction

Consider how characters and creatures interact with the game environment using mocap-based animations. Implement physics-based interactions like climbing, crawling, or grabbing objects.

```
// Implementing physics-based interactions with mocap animations
CharacterInteraction interactionSystem;
```

```
interactionSystem.EnablePhysicsInteractions("Climbing", "Crawling", "ObjectIn
teraction");
```

4.4.12. Export and Integration

Once mocap-enhanced animations are ready, export them in a compatible format (e.g., FBX) and integrate them into CryEngine. Ensure that animations are correctly assigned to characters and creatures.

```
// Exporting and integrating mocap-enhanced animations in CryEngine
CharacterModel character;
character.ExportAndIntegrate("MocapAnimations.fbx");
```

In conclusion, motion capture integration and enhancement are powerful tools for achieving lifelike character animations in CryEngine. This process involves understanding motion capture technology, choosing the right mocap system, setting up mocap sessions, capturing raw data, cleaning and refining data, rigging and retargeting, combining mocap and keyframe animations, facial mocap integration, testing and iteration, optimization and compression, environmental interaction, and export and integration. By mastering these techniques, you can create character animations that enhance the realism and immersion of your game world.

4.5. Detailed Facial Animation and Expression Systems

Facial animations and expressions are essential for conveying emotions and adding depth to characters in video games. In this section, we will explore the intricacies of creating detailed facial animations and expression systems in CryEngine, allowing characters to emote realistically and engage players on a more profound level.

4.5.1. Importance of Facial Animations

Facial animations are a crucial aspect of character design. They enable characters to communicate emotions, reactions, and dialogues effectively. Detailed facial animations enhance the player's connection with the in-game characters.

4.5.2. Facial Rigging

Facial rigging is the foundation of realistic facial animations. It involves creating a skeletal structure for the face, including bones for the eyes, mouth, eyebrows, and other facial features. CryEngine provides tools for setting up facial rigs.

```
// Setting up a facial rig in CryEngine
CharacterFacialRig facialRig;
facialRig.CreateFacialSkeleton("FacialSkeleton");
```

4.5.3. Blendshapes and Morph Targets

Blendshapes or morph targets are essential for controlling different facial expressions. Create a set of blendshapes representing various emotions such as happiness, sadness, anger, and surprise. These blendshapes can be blended together to create a wide range of expressions.

```
// Defining blendshapes for facial expressions in CryEngine
CharacterFacialRig facialRig;
facialRig.CreateBlendshapes("Happiness", "Sadness", "Anger", "Surprise");
```

4.5.4. Lip Syncing

Lip syncing ensures that a character's mouth movements synchronize with spoken dialogues. Implement lip sync systems that analyze speech audio and trigger the appropriate blendshapes for accurate lip movements.

```
// Implementing lip syncing for character dialogues in CryEngine
CharacterFacialRig facialRig;
facialRig.LipSync("AudioAnalysis", "SyncedBlendshapes");
```

4.5.5. Eye Movements

Realistic eye movements are crucial for conveying emotions and attentiveness. Use inverse kinematics (IK) to control the orientation of a character's eyes and eyelids dynamically.

```
// Implementing eye movements with IK for character animations
CharacterFacialRig facialRig;
facialRig.ControlEyeMovements("EyeIK");
```

4.5.6. Blinking and Blink Control

Characters blink to keep their eyes moist and protect them from debris. Implement automatic blinking and manual blink control to achieve natural-looking eye behavior.

```
// Implementing blinking and blink control for characters
CharacterFacialRig facialRig;
facialRig.AutomaticBlinking("EyeBlink");
facialRig.ManualBlinkControl("BlinkButton");
```

4.5.7. Emotion Blending

Create systems that blend multiple blendshapes together to represent complex emotions. For example, a character showing both happiness and surprise might blend the corresponding blendshapes in different proportions.

```
// Blending multiple blendshapes for complex emotional expressions
CharacterFacialRig facialRig;
facialRig.BlendEmotions("Happiness", "Surprise", "ExpressionIntensity");
```

4.5.8. Expressive Dialogues

When characters engage in dialogues, their facial animations should convey not only lip syncing but also subtle expressions that match the tone and content of the conversation.

```
// Creating expressive dialogues with synchronized facial animations
CharacterFacialRig facialRig;
facialRig.SynchronizeDialogues("EmotionMapping", "DialogueText");
```

4.5.9. Interaction with the Environment

Characters' facial expressions should react to their surroundings and events. Implement systems that trigger specific expressions based on in-game events or interactions.

```
// Environmental interaction triggering facial expressions
CharacterFacialRig facialRig;
facialRig.ReactToEnvironment("EventDetection", "ExpressionMapping");
```

4.5.10. Testing and Feedback

Testing facial animations extensively is essential. Use player feedback and playtesting to fine-tune animations and ensure that they effectively convey emotions and reactions.

4.5.11. Performance Optimization

Optimize facial animations for performance, especially in multiplayer or resource-intensive scenarios. Implement level-of-detail (LOD) systems for facial animations to reduce computational load.

```
// Implementing LODs for facial animations in CryEngine
CharacterFacialRig facialRig;
facialRig.CreateLODs("LOD0", "LOD1", "LOD2");
```

4.5.12. Export and Integration

Once facial animations are complete, export them in a compatible format (e.g., FBX) and integrate them into CryEngine. Ensure that animations are correctly assigned to characters, and facial rigs are well-connected.

```
// Exporting and integrating facial animations in CryEngine
CharacterModel character;
character.ExportAndIntegrate("FacialAnimations.fbx");
```

In conclusion, detailed facial animation and expression systems are integral to creating believable and emotionally engaging characters in CryEngine-powered games. This process involves facial rigging, blendshapes and morph targets, lip syncing, eye movements, blinking and blink control, emotion blending, expressive dialogues, interaction with the environment, testing and feedback, performance optimization, and export and integration. By mastering these techniques, you can create characters that not only look realistic but also convey emotions effectively, enhancing the overall gaming experience.

Chapter 5: Advanced Physics and Simulation

5.1. Realistic Physics for Dynamic Gameplay

Realistic physics are crucial for creating immersive and dynamic gameplay experiences in CryEngine. They allow objects, characters, and environments to interact believably, enhancing the overall realism of the game world. In this section, we will delve into the intricacies of implementing realistic physics for dynamic gameplay.

5.1.1. Physics Engines in CryEngine

CryEngine utilizes a powerful physics engine to simulate the behavior of objects and characters within the game world. Understanding and harnessing the capabilities of this physics engine is essential for achieving realism in your game.

```
// Initializing the CryEngine physics engine
PhysicsEngine physicsEngine;
physicsEngine.Initialize("AdvancedSettings");
```

5.1.2. Rigid Body Dynamics

Rigid body dynamics simulate the motion and collisions of solid objects. Objects can have mass, inertia, and collision shapes. Implementing rigid body physics allows for realistic object interactions.

```
// Creating a rigid body for a game object
RigidBodyObject gameObject;
gameObject.SetMass(10.0f);
gameObject.SetCollisionShape("BoxCollider");
```

5.1.3. Constraints and Joints

Constraints and joints enable you to control how objects are connected and behave together. Implement hinge joints, sliders, and other constraints to create complex mechanical systems.

```
// Creating a hinge joint between two objects
PhysicsJoint hingeJoint;
hingeJoint.CreateHingeJoint("ObjectA", "ObjectB", "HingeSettings");
```

5.1.4. Collision Detection and Response

Accurate collision detection and response are fundamental for realistic physics interactions. CryEngine's physics engine handles collision detection and provides callbacks for custom collision responses.

```
// Custom collision response function
void OnCollision(CollisionInfo info) {
    // Handle collision response here
}
```

5.1.5. Character Physics

Incorporate character physics to simulate the movement and interactions of in-game characters. Character physics handle walking, running, jumping, and various animations that respond to the game world.

```
// Implementing character physics for player movement
PlayerCharacter playerCharacter;
playerCharacter.EnableCharacterPhysics("MovementSettings");
```

5.1.6. Ragdoll Physics

Ragdoll physics are crucial for simulating the realistic behavior of characters and creatures when they are defeated or incapacitated. Implementing ragdoll physics adds depth to character animations.

```
// Enabling ragdoll physics for defeated characters
CharacterModel character;
character.EnableRagdollPhysics("RagdollSettings");
```

5.1.7. Vehicle Physics

For games featuring vehicles, implementing accurate vehicle physics is essential. CryEngine provides tools for creating realistic vehicle physics, including suspension, steering, and tire friction.

```
// Setting up realistic physics for a game vehicle
VehiclePhysics vehicle;
vehicle.ConfigurePhysics("SuspensionSettings", "SteeringSettings", "TireFrict
ion");
```

5.1.8. Fluid Dynamics and Water Simulation

For games with water environments, consider implementing fluid dynamics and water simulation. This can include buoyancy, water flow, and realistic interactions between objects and water.

```
// Simulating fluid dynamics and buoyancy in water
WaterSimulation water;
water.EnableFluidDynamics("BuoyancySettings", "FlowSimulation");
```

5.1.9. Dynamic Destruction

Dynamic destruction enhances realism by allowing objects and structures to break apart realistically during explosions or collisions. CryEngine provides tools for implementing dynamic destruction.

```
// Implementing dynamic destruction for game objects
DynamicDestruction destruction;
destruction.EnableDestruction("ExplosionSettings", "CollisionDetection");
```

5.1.10. Testing and Optimization

Thoroughly test the physics interactions in your game to ensure that they align with your design and provide a satisfying player experience. Optimize physics simulations for performance, especially in complex scenes with many interacting objects.

5.1.11. Advanced Physics Interactions

Consider advanced physics interactions, such as soft body dynamics, cloth simulation, and complex materials. These can further enhance the realism and immersion of your game.

```
// Implementing soft body dynamics for deformable objects
SoftBodyObject softBodyObject;
softBodyObject.EnableSoftBodyPhysics("DeformationSettings");
```

5.1.12. Environmental Physics

Integrate environmental physics, such as wind, weather, and terrain deformation, to create a dynamic and evolving game world that responds to player actions and external influences.

```
// Adding environmental physics like wind and terrain deformation
EnvironmentalPhysics environment;
environment.EnableWindSimulation("WindSettings");
environment.EnableTerrainDeformation("DeformationEffects");
```

In conclusion, achieving realistic physics for dynamic gameplay in CryEngine involves understanding the physics engine, implementing rigid body dynamics, constraints and joints, collision detection and response, character physics, ragdoll physics, vehicle physics, fluid dynamics and water simulation, dynamic destruction, testing and optimization, advanced physics interactions, and environmental physics. These elements combine to create a game world where objects, characters, and environments behave believably, enhancing player immersion and engagement.

5.2. Creating Complex Simulations in CryEngine

Creating complex simulations in CryEngine adds depth and realism to your game world, offering players immersive experiences. In this section, we will explore the techniques and tools for designing and implementing intricate simulations within the engine.

5.2.1. Simulation Types

CryEngine supports various types of simulations, including:

- **Physics Simulations:** As discussed in the previous section, CryEngine provides robust physics simulations for objects, characters, and vehicles.

- **Weather and Climate Simulations:** Implementing weather and climate systems allows for dynamic changes in environmental conditions, such as rain, snow, and wind.

- **Ecosystem Simulations:** Creating ecosystems with flora and fauna that interact with each other and the environment can make the game world feel alive.

- **Population and Crowd Simulations:** Populate your game world with crowds of NPCs that behave realistically, adding to the game's immersion.

- **Economic and Trade Simulations:** For strategy or simulation games, implement economic models and trade systems that affect in-game economies.

5.2.2. Weather and Climate Simulation

Implementing weather and climate simulation involves modeling atmospheric conditions, including temperature, humidity, and precipitation. CryEngine's environmental tools can simulate rain, snow, and other weather effects dynamically.

```
// Enabling dynamic weather simulation
WeatherSimulation weather;
weather.EnableDynamicWeather("Temperature", "Humidity", "Precipitation");
```

5.2.3. Ecosystem Simulation

Creating ecosystems in your game world involves defining the interactions between plants, animals, and the environment. This can include predator-prey relationships, plant growth, and environmental changes.

```
// Simulating an ecosystem with predator-prey interactions
EcosystemSimulation ecosystem;
ecosystem.CreateEcosystem("Predators", "Prey", "PlantLife", "EnvironmentalFactors");
```

5.2.4. Population and Crowd Simulation

To populate your game world with NPCs and crowds, consider using population and crowd simulation techniques. These systems can control the behavior and movement of large groups of characters.

```
// Implementing crowd simulation for a city environment
CrowdSimulation crowd;
crowd.CreateCrowd("CityPopulation", "BehavioralRules", "CrowdNavigation");
```

5.2.5. Economic and Trade Simulation

For strategy or simulation games, economic and trade simulations can add depth to gameplay. Create economic models that consider supply, demand, production, and trade routes.

```
// Implementing economic simulation for a trading game
EconomicSimulation economicModel;
economicModel.CreateEconomicModel("SupplyDemand", "Production", "TradeRoutes"
);
```

5.2.6. Realistic Feedback

Ensure that simulations provide realistic feedback to the player. For example, if weather simulations affect gameplay, communicate these changes through visual and auditory cues.

```
// Communicating weather effects through visual and auditory feedback
PlayerHUD playerHUD;
playerHUD.DisplayWeatherAlerts("WeatherEffects");
```

5.2.7. User Interaction

Allow players to interact with simulations when it makes sense in your game. For example, players might influence the ecosystem by hunting or planting trees.

```
// Implementing player interaction with the ecosystem
PlayerCharacter playerCharacter;
playerCharacter.InteractWithEcosystem("Hunting", "Planting");
```

5.2.8. Testing and Balancing

Testing and balancing simulations are crucial. Ensure that simulations do not make the game overly complex or frustrating for players. Adjust simulation parameters to achieve the desired gameplay experience.

5.2.9. Performance Optimization

Optimize simulations for performance, especially when dealing with large-scale simulations or complex interactions. Consider level-of-detail (LOD) techniques and efficient algorithms.

```
// Implementing LODs for population and crowd simulations
CrowdSimulation crowd;
crowd.CreateLODs("HighDetail", "MediumDetail", "LowDetail");
```

5.2.10. Environmental Impact

Consider how simulations impact the game world and its resources. Simulated ecosystems, for example, may affect the availability of resources in the game.

```
// Modeling resource availability based on ecosystem simulations
ResourceManagement resourceManager;
resourceManager.UpdateResourceAvailability("EcosystemImpact");
```

5.2.11. Realism vs. Gameplay

Strike a balance between realism and gameplay. While simulations can enhance realism, they should also contribute positively to the player's experience and not overwhelm them with complexity.

In conclusion, creating complex simulations in CryEngine adds depth, realism, and immersion to your game. These simulations can include weather and climate, ecosystems, populations and crowds, economic models, and more. To implement successful simulations, consider realism, player feedback, user interaction, testing and balancing, performance optimization, environmental impact, and the balance between realism and gameplay. By mastering these techniques, you can create a game world that feels dynamic and alive, enriching the player's experience.

5.3. Cloth, Hair, and Soft Body Dynamics

In this section, we will delve into the implementation of cloth, hair, and soft body dynamics in CryEngine. These simulation techniques add a layer of realism to character and environmental interactions, enhancing the visual and tactile experience in your game.

5.3.1. Cloth Simulation

Cloth simulation involves modeling the behavior of fabrics and textiles. In CryEngine, you can enable cloth simulations for character clothing, flags, banners, and other cloth-like objects.

```
// Enabling cloth simulation for character clothing
CharacterClothing characterClothing;
characterClothing.EnableClothSimulation("ClothSettings");
```

Cloth simulations take into account factors such as gravity, wind, and collisions. The result is natural-looking cloth movement that responds to in-game forces and interactions.

5.3.2. Hair Simulation

Hair simulation is essential for creating realistic hair movement for characters and creatures. It involves modeling individual hair strands and their interactions with the environment.

```
// Implementing hair simulation for character hair
CharacterHair characterHair;
characterHair.EnableHairSimulation("HairSettings");
```

Hair simulations consider factors like gravity, wind, and collision with objects and characters. They result in dynamic and visually appealing hair animations that respond to character movement and environmental conditions.

5.3.3. Soft Body Dynamics

Soft body dynamics simulate the deformation and movement of soft and flexible objects. This includes items like cushions, pillows, and deformable terrain.

```
// Enabling soft body dynamics for deformable terrain
Terrain terrain;
terrain.EnableSoftBodyDynamics("DeformationSettings");
```

Soft body simulations account for forces such as compression, stretching, and bending. Objects with soft body dynamics respond realistically to external forces, enhancing the tactile feel of the game world.

5.3.4. Cloth and Hair Materials

The visual appearance of cloth and hair in simulations is influenced by material properties. Define the material properties, such as stiffness and friction, to control how cloth and hair respond to forces.

```
// Setting material properties for cloth and hair simulations
MaterialProperties clothMaterial;
clothMaterial.SetStiffness(0.8f);
clothMaterial.SetFriction(0.2f);

MaterialProperties hairMaterial;
hairMaterial.SetStiffness(0.6f);
hairMaterial.SetFriction(0.1f);
```

5.3.5. Collision Handling

Handling collisions is crucial in cloth, hair, and soft body simulations. Ensure that these dynamic objects interact believably with the game world, characters, and other physical objects.

```
// Configuring collision handling for cloth and hair simulations
CollisionHandler collisionHandler;
collisionHandler.ConfigureClothCollisions("CharacterCollision", "ObjectCollis
ion");
collisionHandler.ConfigureHairCollisions("CharacterCollision", "EnvironmentCo
llision");
collisionHandler.ConfigureSoftBodyCollisions("TerrainCollision", "ObjectColli
sion");
```

5.3.6. Performance Optimization

Optimizing cloth, hair, and soft body simulations is essential for maintaining good performance. Consider using level-of-detail (LOD) techniques to reduce computational load when these dynamic elements are not in close view of the camera.

```
// Implementing LODs for cloth, hair, and soft body simulations
CharacterClothing characterClothing;
```

```
characterClothing.CreateLODs("HighDetail", "MediumDetail", "LowDetail");

CharacterHair characterHair;
characterHair.CreateLODs("HighDetail", "MediumDetail", "LowDetail");

Terrain terrain;
terrain.CreateLODs("HighDetail", "MediumDetail", "LowDetail");
```

5.3.7. Realism and Player Interaction

Balancing realism and player interaction is essential. While realistic cloth, hair, and soft body dynamics enhance the visual experience, they should also respond appropriately to player actions, ensuring a satisfying gameplay experience.

```
// Implementing player interactions with cloth and soft body objects
PlayerCharacter playerCharacter;
playerCharacter.InteractWithCloth("GrabCloth");
playerCharacter.InteractWithSoftBody("SqueezePillow");
```

5.3.8. Testing and Fine-Tuning

Testing cloth, hair, and soft body simulations thoroughly is crucial. Adjust material properties, collision handling, and other parameters to achieve the desired visual and physical behavior.

In conclusion, implementing cloth, hair, and soft body dynamics in CryEngine allows you to create visually stunning and physically immersive experiences for players. These simulations add realism to character clothing, hair, and deformable objects in the game world. By configuring material properties, handling collisions, optimizing performance, and balancing realism with player interaction, you can achieve dynamic and visually appealing results that enhance the overall gaming experience.

5.4. Implementing Destructible Environments

Implementing destructible environments in CryEngine can significantly enhance gameplay by allowing structures and objects to break apart realistically during explosions, collisions, or other destructive events. In this section, we will explore the techniques and tools for achieving destructible environments within the engine.

5.4.1. Destructible Objects

Destructible objects are assets that can be fractured or broken into smaller pieces during gameplay. These objects can range from buildings and structures to everyday items.

```
// Creating a destructible building object
DestructibleObject building;
```

```
building.SetMesh("BuildingMesh");
building.EnableDestruction("DestructionSettings");
```

5.4.2. Destruction Models

To implement destructible environments, you need to define destruction models for objects. These models specify how an object breaks apart, the fracture patterns, and the forces required for destruction.

```
// Defining a destruction model for a wooden crate
DestructionModel crateDestruction;
crateDestruction.SetFracturePattern("WoodenPattern");
crateDestruction.SetDestructionForce(5000.0f);
```

5.4.3. Physics-Based Simulation

Destruction in CryEngine is physics-based, meaning that objects respond to forces and interactions realistically. Explosions, collisions, or other forces can trigger the destruction of objects.

```
// Applying an explosion force to trigger destruction
Explosion explosion;
explosion.ApplyExplosionForce("ExplosionSettings", "Building");
```

5.4.4. Particle Effects

To enhance the visual impact of destruction, consider adding particle effects such as dust, debris, and smoke. These effects make the destruction of objects more visually appealing and immersive.

```
// Emitting particle effects during object destruction
ParticleEmitter debrisEmitter;
debrisEmitter.EmitDebrisParticles("DebrisEffect", "BuildingFractures");
```

5.4.5. Sound Effects

Sound effects play a crucial role in conveying the sense of destruction. Implement sound cues that correspond to the destruction events, such as crumbling, crashing, or explosions.

```
// Playing sound effects during object destruction
SoundEffects soundEffects;
soundEffects.PlayDestructionSounds("BuildingCollapseSounds");
```

5.4.6. Destruction Events

Destruction events should be triggered by in-game events, such as a player's actions or scripted events. You can set up scripts or gameplay logic to initiate destruction sequences.

```
// Triggering destruction events based on player actions
PlayerCharacter playerCharacter;
playerCharacter.TriggerDestructionEvent("DestroyBuilding");
```

5.4.7. Level Design Considerations

When designing levels with destructible environments, think about how destruction impacts gameplay. It can open up new pathways, create cover, or change the flow of a level.

```
// Designing levels with destructible objects as gameplay elements
LevelDesign levelDesign;
levelDesign.IncorporateDestruction("DestructibleObstacles", "StrategicCover")
;
```

5.4.8. Performance Optimization

Optimizing the performance of destructible environments is crucial, especially in scenes with many destructible objects. Implement LOD (level-of-detail) techniques and use efficient algorithms for destruction physics.

```
// Implementing LODs for destructible objects
DestructibleObject building;
building.CreateLODs("HighDetail", "MediumDetail", "LowDetail");
```

5.4.9. Balancing Gameplay

Balancing gameplay involving destructible environments is essential. Ensure that destruction events are challenging but fair, and that they enhance rather than disrupt the overall gaming experience.

5.4.10. Testing and Iteration

Thoroughly test and iterate on destructible environments to ensure that they align with your game's design and provide a satisfying player experience. Fine-tune destruction models, physics parameters, and visual effects as needed.

In conclusion, implementing destructible environments in CryEngine adds an exciting layer of realism and interactivity to your game. Destructible objects respond to forces realistically, and you can enhance the visual and auditory experience with particle effects and sound cues. When designing levels with destructible environments, consider their impact on gameplay and balance, and optimize for performance. By mastering these techniques, you can create immersive and dynamic game worlds where destruction is not only visually stunning but also an integral part of the gameplay experience.

5.5. Fluid Dynamics and Real-Time Effects

Fluid dynamics and real-time effects play a significant role in creating realistic and immersive game worlds in CryEngine. In this section, we will explore how to implement fluid simulations and real-time effects to enhance the visual and interactive aspects of your game.

5.5.1. Fluid Simulations

Fluid simulations involve modeling the behavior of liquids and gases, such as water, smoke, and fire. CryEngine provides tools to simulate and render these elements realistically.

```
// Implementing fluid simulation for water surfaces
WaterSimulation water;
water.EnableWaterSimulation("WaterSettings");
```

Fluid simulations take into account factors like viscosity, density, and surface tension to create lifelike fluid movement and interactions with objects and characters.

5.5.2. Real-Time Effects

Real-time effects include a wide range of visual and interactive elements, from dynamic lighting and particle effects to weather changes and environmental interactions.

```
// Implementing real-time weather changes
WeatherSystem weatherSystem;
weatherSystem.EnableDynamicWeatherChanges("WeatherSettings");
```

Real-time effects can significantly impact gameplay and player immersion by providing dynamic and responsive elements in the game world.

5.5.3. Particle Systems

Particle systems are a fundamental tool for creating various real-time effects, including fire, smoke, sparks, and magical spells. These systems emit and control particles that simulate these visual phenomena.

```
// Emitting fire particles for a torch
ParticleEmitter fireEmitter;
fireEmitter.EmitFireParticles("TorchFireEffect");
```

Particle systems allow you to define particle behavior, appearance, and interactions with the environment.

5.5.4. Dynamic Lighting

Dynamic lighting enhances the visual quality of your game by simulating realistic lighting conditions. This includes real-time shadows, reflections, and global illumination.

```
// Implementing dynamic lighting with global illumination
DynamicLighting lighting;
lighting.EnableGlobalIllumination("LightingSettings");
```

Dynamic lighting affects the way objects and characters are lit and shaded in real-time, adding depth and realism to the game's visuals.

5.5.5. Environmental Interactions

Environmental interactions involve objects and characters responding to the game world's dynamic elements. For example, characters may leave footprints in the snow, or objects may float in water.

```
// Implementing environmental interactions like footprints in snow
Character character;
character.LeaveFootprints("SnowFootprints");
```

Environmental interactions make the game world feel alive and responsive to player actions.

5.5.6. Audio Synchronization

Syncing audio with real-time effects is essential for creating an immersive experience. Sound cues should align with visual effects and gameplay events.

```
// Synchronizing audio with real-time effects
SoundEffects soundEffects;
soundEffects.SyncAudioWithVisuals("ExplosionSounds", "ExplosionEffects");
```

Audio synchronization enhances the overall impact of real-time effects on player immersion.

5.5.7. Performance Considerations

Real-time effects and fluid simulations can be computationally intensive. Implement performance optimization techniques, such as level-of-detail (LOD) and culling, to maintain a smooth gaming experience.

```
// Implementing LODs for particle systems and fluid simulations
ParticleEmitter particleEmitter;
particleEmitter.CreateLODs("HighDetail", "MediumDetail", "LowDetail");

WaterSimulation water;
water.CreateLODs("HighDetail", "MediumDetail", "LowDetail");
```

5.5.8. Gameplay Integration

Integrate real-time effects and fluid simulations into your gameplay mechanics to create engaging and interactive experiences. For example, using fire and water mechanics for puzzles or combat situations.

```
// Incorporating fire and water mechanics into gameplay
GameplayMechanics mechanics;
mechanics.CreateFirePuzzle("FirePuzzle");
mechanics.ImplementWaterCombat("WaterCombat");
```

5.5.9. Testing and Iteration

Thoroughly test and iterate on fluid simulations and real-time effects to ensure they align with your game's design and provide an immersive player experience. Fine-tune parameters and interactions as needed.

In conclusion, fluid dynamics and real-time effects are powerful tools for enhancing the visual and interactive aspects of your game in CryEngine. Whether simulating realistic fluids, creating dynamic lighting, or integrating environmental interactions, these elements contribute to a more immersive and engaging player experience. By effectively implementing and balancing these techniques, you can create game worlds that feel alive and responsive, enriching the overall gaming experience.

Chapter 6: Cutting-Edge Graphics and Visual Effects

Section 6.1: Advanced Shader Programming and Material Design

In the world of game development, creating stunning visuals and immersive environments is paramount. To achieve this, mastering advanced shader programming and material design is crucial. This section delves into the intricacies of these topics, providing you with the knowledge and techniques to take your game's graphics to the next level.

Understanding Shaders

Shaders are the building blocks of modern game graphics. They control how light interacts with objects, surfaces, and materials in your game world. Advanced shader programming involves creating custom shaders that go beyond the basics. These shaders can simulate complex effects such as realistic water reflections, dynamic lighting, and intricate material properties.

```
// Example of a custom shader code
float4 main(float4 color : COLOR) : SV_Target
{
    // Your shader logic here
    // This can include calculations for lighting, reflections, and more.
    return color;
}
```

Material Design and Textures

Materials define how surfaces appear in your game. They encompass properties like color, reflectivity, roughness, and transparency. Advanced material design involves crafting materials that respond realistically to environmental factors. This might include creating materials that change appearance when wet, become damaged, or react to different lighting conditions.

```
-- Lua script for material properties
material = {
    diffuseColor = {0.8, 0.2, 0.2},
    specularColor = {0.9, 0.9, 0.9},
    roughness = 0.2,
    -- Additional material properties go here
}
```

Shader Techniques

Advanced shader techniques allow you to achieve stunning visual effects. Some examples include:

- **Parallax Mapping**: Simulating 3D depth on flat surfaces to create intricate surface details.

- **Screen Space Reflections (SSR)**: Realistic reflections that dynamically adapt to the game environment.
- **Post-Processing Effects**: Adding depth of field, motion blur, and other effects to enhance realism.

These techniques often require a deep understanding of shader languages like HLSL (High-Level Shading Language) or GLSL (OpenGL Shading Language).

GPU Optimization

Creating advanced shaders and materials can be resource-intensive. Optimizing your shaders to run efficiently on the GPU (Graphics Processing Unit) is vital for maintaining smooth gameplay. This involves techniques like minimizing redundant calculations, using LOD (Level of Detail) techniques, and efficiently managing texture memory.

```
// Optimized shader code
void main()
{
    // Efficient shader logic here
    // Minimize unnecessary calculations for better performance.
}
```

Real-Time Feedback and Testing

As you develop advanced shaders and materials, real-time feedback and testing become essential. CryEngine provides tools and debugging capabilities to visualize shader effects and tweak material properties in real-time. This iterative process allows you to fine-tune your graphics until they meet your desired visual quality.

In conclusion, mastering advanced shader programming and material design is fundamental for creating visually stunning and immersive game environments. Understanding shaders, materials, optimization techniques, and real-time testing will empower you to push the boundaries of what's possible in game graphics. This knowledge is a valuable asset for any game developer looking to create cutting-edge visual experiences.

Section 6.2: Implementing Ray Tracing and Global Illumination

Ray tracing and global illumination are advanced rendering techniques that have revolutionized the realism of computer-generated graphics in recent years. This section explores the integration of ray tracing and global illumination into your CryEngine projects, enhancing the visual fidelity of your games.

Understanding Ray Tracing

Ray tracing is a rendering technique that simulates the path of light rays as they interact with surfaces in a virtual environment. Unlike traditional rasterization techniques, ray tracing calculates the interactions of each ray individually, allowing for accurate reflections, refractions, and shadows. It creates a level of visual realism that was previously challenging to achieve.

```
// Ray tracing example code
Ray ray = createRayFromCamera(screenX, screenY);
Intersection intersection = traceRay(ray);
Color pixelColor = shadeIntersection(intersection);
```

Benefits of Ray Tracing

- **Realistic Reflections**: Ray tracing enables accurate reflections on surfaces, including mirror-like reflections and reflections on curved objects.
- **Refractions**: Transparent materials can refract light realistically, creating effects like caustics and underwater distortion.
- **Soft Shadows**: Ray tracing produces soft and natural-looking shadows with soft edges, eliminating the need for shadow maps.
- **Global Illumination**: Ray tracing facilitates global illumination, which accurately simulates how light bounces and affects the overall lighting in a scene.

Global Illumination Techniques

Global illumination (GI) refers to the simulation of indirect lighting in a scene. It accounts for light bouncing off surfaces and affecting the color and brightness of other objects. CryEngine offers several GI techniques:

- **Radiosity**: Radiosity is a classic GI technique that calculates indirect lighting by subdividing surfaces into small patches and simulating the transfer of light between them.
- **Photon Mapping**: Photon mapping uses emitted photons to simulate indirect lighting and is particularly effective for complex scenes with many light sources.
- **Path Tracing**: Path tracing traces rays of light as they bounce around the scene, making it one of the most physically accurate GI methods.

```
-- CryEngine GI settings
GI = {
    method = "Path Tracing",
    samples = 1000,
    bounceLimit = 8,
    -- Additional GI parameters can be configured here
}
```

Implementation Considerations

Integrating ray tracing and global illumination into your CryEngine project requires careful consideration of performance and hardware requirements. While modern GPUs are capable of ray tracing, optimizing your scenes and settings is crucial to maintaining a playable frame rate.

Furthermore, CryEngine provides a user-friendly interface for configuring ray tracing and GI settings, making it accessible to developers without an in-depth understanding of the underlying algorithms.

In conclusion, implementing ray tracing and global illumination in CryEngine can significantly elevate the visual quality of your games. These techniques enable realistic lighting, shadows, and reflections, contributing to a more immersive player experience. While they may introduce additional computational demands, the visual benefits they provide are well worth the investment for developers aiming to create visually stunning and lifelike game worlds.

Section 6.3: High-Dynamic-Range Imaging (HDRI) Techniques

High-Dynamic-Range Imaging (HDRI) is a crucial aspect of modern game graphics that allows for more realistic and visually appealing scenes. This section explores the concepts and techniques behind HDRI and how to implement them effectively in CryEngine.

Understanding High-Dynamic-Range Imaging (HDRI)

HDRI refers to the capture, storage, and rendering of images with a wider range of luminance values than standard images. In traditional images, details in extremely bright or dark areas can be lost due to the limited dynamic range. HDRI, on the other hand, retains this information, allowing for more accurate and visually pleasing lighting and reflections in your games.

Benefits of HDRI

- **Realistic Lighting**: HDRI provides the foundation for accurate and realistic lighting in your game world. It captures the subtle nuances of real-world lighting conditions.
- **Dynamic Range**: With HDRI, you can represent a broader range of light intensities, from the dim glow of a candle to the brilliance of sunlight, resulting in more lifelike scenes.
- **Image-Based Lighting (IBL)**: HDRI images are commonly used for IBL, where the captured environment map is used to illuminate 3D scenes convincingly.

```
// HDRI usage example in CryEngine
EnvironmentMap hdriMap("forest_hill.hdr");
hdriMap.applyToScene();
```

Capturing HDRI Images

To utilize HDRI effectively, you need high-quality HDRI images. These images are typically captured using specialized cameras or created by merging multiple exposures of the same scene. The result is a 32-bit per channel image, which stores a wide range of brightness values.

Implementing HDRI in CryEngine

CryEngine supports HDRI seamlessly, allowing you to apply HDRI environment maps to your scenes. You can use HDRI maps to provide realistic lighting and reflections in your game world. CryEngine's physically-based rendering (PBR) system is particularly compatible with HDRI, as it accurately simulates the interaction of light with materials.

```
-- CryEngine HDRI settings
EnvironmentMap = {
    map = "desert_sunset.hdr",
    intensity = 2.0,
    reflectionIntensity = 1.5,
    -- Additional HDRI parameters can be configured here
}
```

HDRI for Reflections

One significant application of HDRI is in creating convincing reflections on surfaces. By using HDRI maps as reflection cubemaps, you can achieve lifelike reflections that adapt to the environment. This is especially valuable for reflective materials like water or metallic surfaces.

Performance Considerations

While HDRI greatly enhances visual quality, it can also be computationally demanding. Developers need to strike a balance between visual fidelity and performance, especially on lower-end hardware. CryEngine provides settings and options to control the intensity of HDRI and reflections, allowing you to optimize for different target platforms.

In conclusion, High-Dynamic-Range Imaging (HDRI) is a vital component of modern game graphics, enabling realistic lighting, reflections, and dynamic range. By understanding the principles of HDRI and how to implement them effectively in CryEngine, you can elevate the visual quality of your games, creating more immersive and visually stunning environments for players to explore.

Section 6.4: Particle Systems and Visual Effect Enhancements

Particle systems are a fundamental component of modern game development, allowing you to create a wide range of visual effects that enhance gameplay and immersion. In this section, we will explore how to leverage particle systems and other techniques to enhance visual effects in CryEngine.

Particle Systems in CryEngine

CryEngine provides a robust and versatile particle system that enables you to create a variety of visual effects, including fire, smoke, explosions, rain, and more. These particle systems are composed of individual particles, each with properties like position, velocity, size, and color.

```
<!-- CryEngine Particle System Definition -->
<ParticleEmitter>
    <Effect>fire</Effect>
    <MaxParticles>100</MaxParticles>
    <Lifetime>2.0</Lifetime>
    <!-- Additional particle system parameters -->
</ParticleEmitter>
```

Key Concepts in Particle Systems

- **Emitters**: Emitters release particles into the game world. Each emitter can have its own set of properties, such as particle type, rate of emission, and direction.

- **Particles**: Particles are individual elements within a particle system. They can represent objects like sparks, debris, or raindrops. Particles can be customized with various attributes.

- **Forces**: Forces can affect the behavior of particles. Common forces include gravity, wind, and turbulence, allowing you to create realistic motion for particles.

Particle Effects for Realism

To enhance realism in your game, it's crucial to pay attention to the details of particle effects. For example, in a fire effect, particles should have varying sizes, colors, and lifetimes. Smoke particles should dissipate over time, and sparks should emit light and flicker realistically.

```
// Example code for controlling particle behavior
ParticleEmitter* fireEmitter = createFireEmitter();
fireEmitter->setParticleSize(0.05, 0.2);
fireEmitter->setColor(RGB(255, 100, 0), RGB(255, 0, 0));
fireEmitter->setLifetime(1.0, 3.0);
```

Visual Effect Enhancements

In addition to particle systems, CryEngine offers various techniques to enhance visual effects:

- **Screen Space Reflections (SSR)**: SSR enhances reflections by simulating them in screen space, creating more accurate and visually appealing surfaces.

- **Bloom**: Bloom adds a soft glow to bright areas, creating a visually pleasing and realistic effect for intense light sources.

- **Depth of Field (DOF)**: DOF blurs the background or foreground of the camera focus point, mimicking real-world camera behavior and improving the cinematic quality of your game.

- **Motion Blur**: Motion blur adds realism by blurring objects in motion, simulating the way a camera captures fast movements.

```
-- CryEngine visual effect settings
VisualEffects = {
    SSR = true,
    Bloom = true,
    DOF = true,
    MotionBlur = true,
    -- Additional visual effect parameters can be configured here
}
```

Performance Considerations

While visual effects significantly enhance the player experience, they can also impact performance. It's essential to optimize particle systems and visual effects for different target platforms. CryEngine provides tools and settings to control the quality and performance impact of these effects, ensuring that your game runs smoothly on a variety of hardware.

In conclusion, leveraging particle systems and visual effect enhancements in CryEngine can elevate the visual quality and realism of your games. By understanding the principles of particle systems, fine-tuning their properties, and combining them with other visual effect techniques, you can create immersive and visually stunning game worlds that captivate players and enhance gameplay.

Section 6.5: Real-Time Rendering Optimization Strategies

Optimizing real-time rendering is a critical aspect of game development, ensuring that your game runs smoothly while delivering stunning visuals. In this section, we will explore various strategies and techniques for optimizing real-time rendering in CryEngine.

Importance of Real-Time Rendering Optimization

Optimization is essential because it directly impacts the player's experience. Smooth and consistent frame rates are crucial for immersion and playability. Optimization becomes even more critical as games become more complex, with larger and more detailed environments and more sophisticated visual effects.

Profiling and Performance Analysis

Before diving into optimization strategies, it's essential to profile your game to identify performance bottlenecks. CryEngine provides built-in profiling tools that allow you to monitor CPU and GPU usage, memory consumption, and frame rendering times. Profiling helps you pinpoint areas that need optimization.

```
-- CryEngine profiling example
Profiling = {
    CPU = true,
    GPU = true,
    Memory = true,
    -- Additional profiling settings can be configured here
}
```

Level of Detail (LOD) Systems

LOD systems are a fundamental optimization technique. They involve using lower-detail models or textures for objects that are distant from the camera. CryEngine supports LOD systems, allowing you to create multiple levels of detail for assets and automatically switch between them based on distance.

```
<!-- CryEngine LOD settings -->
<LOD>
    <DistanceRatio>2.0</DistanceRatio>
    <LodModel>low_detail.cgf</LodModel>
</LOD>
```

Occlusion Culling

Occlusion culling is another critical optimization technique. It involves not rendering objects that are not visible to the camera. CryEngine utilizes both static and dynamic occlusion culling methods to reduce unnecessary rendering.

```
// CryEngine occlusion culling settings
OcclusionCulling = {
    StaticOcclusion = true,
    DynamicOcclusion = true,
    -- Additional occlusion culling parameters can be configured here
}
```

Shader and Material Optimization

Optimizing shaders and materials is vital for GPU performance. Consider techniques like shader instancing, which allows multiple objects to share a single shader instance, reducing CPU overhead. Additionally, minimize overdraw by avoiding unnecessary rendering passes and shader complexity.

Batched Rendering

Batching is a technique where you group together similar objects to reduce draw calls. CryEngine provides tools to batch render objects efficiently, improving CPU performance and reducing the overhead of issuing draw calls.

```
// Batched rendering in CryEngine
BatchedRendering = {
    BatchObjects = true,
    -- Additional batched rendering settings can be configured here
}
```

Multi-Threading

CryEngine supports multi-threading, allowing you to offload CPU work to multiple threads. Utilize multi-threading for tasks like physics simulation, AI calculations, and other CPU-intensive processes to maximize CPU utilization and improve overall performance.

```
-- CryEngine multi-threading settings
MultiThreading = {
    Physics = true,
    AI = true,
    -- Additional multi-threading configurations can be specified here
}
```

Cross-Platform Optimization

Optimizing for multiple platforms is a crucial consideration. Different platforms may have varying levels of hardware capabilities. CryEngine allows you to adjust settings and assets to optimize performance for specific platforms, ensuring a consistent experience for players.

In conclusion, real-time rendering optimization is an ongoing process that significantly impacts the performance and visual quality of your game. By profiling your game, implementing LOD systems, occlusion culling, optimizing shaders and materials, using batched rendering, leveraging multi-threading, and tailoring optimizations for specific platforms, you can create a smooth and visually impressive gaming experience that reaches a broader audience.

Section 7.1: Advanced Sound Design and 3D Audio Techniques

Sound design is a crucial aspect of game development, as it enhances immersion and player engagement. In this section, we will delve into advanced sound design techniques and explore 3D audio implementation in CryEngine.

The Importance of Sound Design

Effective sound design can significantly impact a player's emotional connection to a game. It helps establish the game's atmosphere, conveys important information, and adds realism to the experience. In a dynamic and interactive environment, sound can guide players, warn them of danger, and provide feedback on their actions.

Audio Asset Creation

Creating high-quality audio assets is the foundation of sound design. CryEngine supports various audio formats, including WAV, MP3, and OGG. When designing audio assets, consider factors such as bit rate, sample rate, and compression to achieve the best balance between audio quality and file size.

```
# CryEngine audio asset settings
AudioAssets = {
    Format = "WAV",
    BitRate = "16-bit",
    SampleRate = "44100 Hz",
}
```

Dynamic Soundscapes

CryEngine allows for dynamic soundscapes that respond to the game's events and environment. You can use triggers, scripting, and AI-driven events to create immersive audio experiences. For example, the sound of wind in the trees might change as the weather worsens, or footsteps could vary based on the character's movement speed.

```
-- Dynamic soundscape in CryEngine
Soundscapes = {
    ForestAmbience = {
        Weather = {
            Clear = "forest_clear.ogg",
            Rain = "forest_rain.ogg",
            -- More sound variations based on weather can be defined here
        },
    },
}
```

3D Audio and Positional Sound

CryEngine supports 3D audio, which means that sounds are spatially positioned within the game world. This adds depth and realism to the auditory experience. Sound sources can have positions and orientations, and the engine calculates how they should be heard based on the player's location and orientation.

```
-- 3D audio settings in CryEngine
Sound3D = {
    PositionalSound = true,
    DistanceModel = "InverseSquare",
```

```
    -- Additional 3D audio configurations can be specified here
}
```

Realistic Sound Propagation

Sound propagation simulates how sounds travel through the game world. It takes into account factors like obstacles, materials, and environmental conditions. CryEngine's sound propagation system allows for realistic sound behavior, including echoes, reflections, and dampening.

```
// CryEngine sound propagation settings
SoundPropagation = {
    Echo = true,
    Reflections = true,
    Occlusion = true,
    -- Additional sound propagation parameters can be configured here
}
```

Adaptive and Dynamic Soundtracks

Adaptive soundtracks adjust to the player's actions and the game's context. CryEngine supports dynamic music systems that seamlessly transition between different tracks or adapt the music's intensity based on the situation, enhancing immersion and player engagement.

```
-- Adaptive soundtrack scripting in CryEngine
function OnPlayerEnteredCombat()
    -- Switch to combat music
    PlayMusic("combat_music.ogg")
end

function OnPlayerExitedCombat()
    -- Return to exploration music
    PlayMusic("exploration_music.ogg")
end
```

Audio Middleware Integration

CryEngine can integrate with audio middleware solutions like Wwise and FMOD. These tools offer advanced audio authoring and processing capabilities, allowing for even more intricate sound design and audio-driven gameplay experiences.

```
// CryEngine audio middleware integration settings
AudioMiddleware = {
    Integration = "Wwise",
    -- Additional integration configurations can be specified here
}
```

In conclusion, advanced sound design and 3D audio techniques are integral to creating immersive and engaging gaming experiences. By focusing on audio asset quality, implementing dynamic soundscapes, leveraging 3D audio and positional sound, simulating realistic sound propagation, using adaptive and dynamic soundtracks, and integrating audio middleware, you can enhance your game's audio to captivate players and immerse them in your virtual world.

Section 7.2: Implementing Adaptive and Dynamic Soundtracks

In this section, we will explore the implementation of adaptive and dynamic soundtracks in CryEngine. Adaptive soundtracks are an essential element of modern game audio, as they enhance player immersion and create a dynamic emotional connection to the game world.

The Role of Adaptive Soundtracks

Adaptive soundtracks are designed to respond to the player's actions, the game's context, and the overall narrative. They can dynamically change the music based on the player's location, in-game events, or the emotional state of the game's story. This dynamic music enhances the player's engagement and emotional connection to the game.

Musical Layers and Stems

To create adaptive soundtracks, game developers often compose music in layers or stems. Each layer represents a different musical element, such as melody, harmony, percussion, or ambient sounds. These layers can be mixed in real-time to create a seamless and adaptive musical experience.

```
<!-- CryEngine musical layer definitions -->
<Layers>
    <Layer name="Melody" volume="0.8" />
    <Layer name="Percussion" volume="0.6" />
    <Layer name="Ambient" volume="0.5" />
</Layers>
```

Interactive Music States

CryEngine supports the concept of interactive music states. These states define different situations in the game, such as exploration, combat, or suspenseful moments. Each state can have its own set of musical layers and transitions, allowing for smooth and context-aware music changes.

```
-- Defining interactive music states in CryEngine
MusicStates = {
    Exploration = {
        Layers = {
            Melody = "exploration_melody.ogg",
            Percussion = "exploration_percussion.ogg",
            Ambient = "exploration_ambient.ogg",
        },
```

```
        Transitions = {
            Combat = "transition_to_combat.ogg",
        },
    },
    Combat = {
        Layers = {
            Melody = "combat_melody.ogg",
            Percussion = "combat_percussion.ogg",
            Ambient = "combat_ambient.ogg",
        },
        Transitions = {
            Exploration = "transition_to_exploration.ogg",
        },
    },
}
```

Crossfading and Transition Logic

To achieve smooth transitions between different music states, CryEngine provides crossfading and transition logic. Crossfading gradually blends the audio layers when transitioning between states, ensuring a seamless listening experience for players.

```
-- Crossfading and transition logic in CryEngine
function OnPlayerEnteredCombat()
    CrossfadeMusic("Combat", 2.0) -- Crossfade to combat music in 2 seconds
end

function OnPlayerExitedCombat()
    CrossfadeMusic("Exploration", 3.0) -- Crossfade to exploration music in 3
seconds
end
```

Emotional Impact

Adaptive soundtracks can have a profound emotional impact on players. They can intensify the excitement during action-packed sequences, create tension in suspenseful moments, or evoke nostalgia during exploration. By carefully designing adaptive soundtracks, game developers can enhance the player's emotional journey and create memorable gaming experiences.

Player Feedback

When implementing adaptive soundtracks, it's essential to gather player feedback and playtest the game thoroughly. Players' reactions to music transitions and their emotional responses should be considered when fine-tuning the soundtrack system. This iterative process helps ensure that the adaptive soundtrack enhances rather than distracts from the gaming experience.

Conclusion

Implementing adaptive and dynamic soundtracks in CryEngine adds a layer of depth and immersion to your game. By creating musical layers and stems, defining interactive music states, using crossfading and transition logic, and considering player feedback, you can craft a captivating auditory experience that enhances your game's narrative and emotional impact. Adaptive soundtracks are a powerful tool to engage players and make your game's world come alive through music.

Section 7.3: Voice Over Recording and Integration

In this section, we delve into the intricate process of voice-over recording and integration in CryEngine. Voice acting is a vital component of game development, as it brings characters to life, delivers narrative depth, and enriches the player's immersion. Effective voice-over integration ensures that dialogues and interactions seamlessly blend with the game's environment.

Preparing for Voice Over

Before recording voiceovers, thorough preparation is essential. Begin by scripting dialogues and character interactions, providing actors with context and emotional nuances for their performances. Create character profiles, voice reference samples, and detailed character briefs to guide actors in embodying their roles effectively.

Professional Recording Setup

Ensure a professional recording environment with high-quality microphones, soundproofing, and audio interfaces. Select experienced voice actors who can convey the desired emotions and personalities of your characters. During recording sessions, provide clear direction and constructive feedback to achieve the best performances.

Scripting and Localization

Write dialogues with localization in mind, allowing for translations and adaptations into different languages. Ensure that your game engine, such as CryEngine, supports localization, and implement a system for managing voice-over assets in multiple languages.

Voice-Over Editing and Cleanup

After recording, voice-over files may require editing and cleanup to remove noise, normalize audio levels, and correct any imperfections. CryEngine provides tools and plugins for audio editing and post-production, allowing you to fine-tune voice-over assets for optimal in-game integration.

Implementing Voice Overs in CryEngine

Integrating voice-overs in CryEngine involves importing voice assets, associating them with characters or objects, and synchronizing them with in-game events and animations. CryEngine's audio middleware supports various formats, ensuring compatibility with industry-standard audio software.

```
<!-- CryEngine XML script for associating voice-over assets -->
<DialogueEvent
    id="npc_dialogue"
    actor="NPC_John"
    audioFile="john_dialogue_01.ogg"
    subtitleFile="john_dialogue_01.srt"
    startEvent="player_approaches_npc"
    endEvent="dialogue_complete"
    loop="false"
/>
```

Lip Sync and Facial Animation

For a realistic in-game experience, sync character lip movements and facial animations with voice-over dialogues. CryEngine's facial animation tools enable precise synchronization, enhancing the believability of character interactions.

Player Choices and Consequences

Consider branching dialogues and player choices that affect the game's narrative. Implement systems to handle multiple dialogue outcomes based on player decisions, ensuring a dynamic and immersive storytelling experience.

Testing and Iteration

Thoroughly playtest voice-over integration to identify any issues, such as audio synchronization problems or awkward transitions. Iterate on the voice-over implementation to address feedback and improve the overall experience.

Accessibility Features

Inclusivity is essential in modern game development. Provide accessibility options such as subtitles and customizable audio settings to accommodate players with different needs and preferences.

Conclusion

Voice-over recording and integration are integral aspects of creating immersive and narrative-rich gaming experiences. By preparing diligently, maintaining a professional recording setup, scripting for localization, editing voice assets, and effectively implementing voice overs in CryEngine, you can elevate the storytelling and character depth in your game. Attention to detail, player choices, and accessibility features contribute to a captivating and inclusive gaming experience.

Section 7.4: Audio Synchronization with Game Events

Audio synchronization plays a crucial role in enhancing the immersive quality of a game. When audio aligns seamlessly with in-game events and actions, it creates a more realistic and engaging experience for players. In this section, we will explore techniques and best practices for synchronizing audio with various game events using CryEngine.

Event-Driven Audio

CryEngine allows developers to trigger audio events based on in-game actions and events. These events can range from a character's footsteps to explosions, ambient sounds, and dialogues. By associating specific audio cues with relevant events, you can create a dynamic and responsive audio environment.

Using CryEngine's Audio Middleware

CryEngine integrates with audio middleware solutions like Audiokinetic Wwise and FMOD Studio. These middleware tools offer advanced audio capabilities, including real-time audio processing, dynamic mixing, and event-driven audio triggering. By utilizing these tools, you can achieve precise audio synchronization and control.

Implementing Audio Triggers

To synchronize audio with game events, you'll need to implement audio triggers in your CryEngine project. These triggers can be defined in the game's scripting language and associated with specific events or actions. When triggered, they play corresponding audio assets, enhancing the player's experience.

```lua
-- Lua script for triggering audio when a player fires a weapon
function OnPlayerShoot()
    Audio.PlayEvent("weapon_fire")
end
```

Dynamic Mixing and Audio States

CryEngine supports dynamic audio mixing, allowing you to adjust audio levels, effects, and spatialization based on the game's context. Implement audio states that change dynamically as the game progresses. For example, you can simulate underwater audio effects when a character dives into water or intensify music during combat sequences.

Spatial Audio and 3D Positioning

Spatial audio enhances realism by simulating sound direction and distance in 3D space. CryEngine offers spatial audio features that enable you to position audio sources within the game world accurately. This is particularly useful for creating immersive environmental audio, where sounds react realistically to the player's movement and orientation.

Audio Layering and Ambiance

Layering audio tracks and ambient sounds can add depth and richness to your game's audio environment. For instance, you can combine background music, environmental sounds, and character dialogues to create a cohesive and immersive auditory experience. Careful layering and mixing are key to achieving this effect.

Testing and Feedback

Thorough testing is essential to ensure that audio synchronization aligns with game events correctly. Playtest the game and gather feedback from players to identify any synchronization issues or areas for improvement. Iteration based on feedback can lead to a more polished audio experience.

Accessibility Considerations

Incorporate accessibility features related to audio synchronization, such as subtitles or visual cues for important audio events. This ensures that players with hearing impairments can still enjoy and understand the game.

Conclusion

Audio synchronization is a critical component of game development that enhances immersion and player engagement. By using event-driven audio triggers, leveraging CryEngine's audio middleware integration, implementing dynamic mixing and spatial audio, and considering accessibility, you can create a compelling and synchronized audio experience in your CryEngine project. Careful attention to audio details contributes significantly to the overall quality of your game.

Section 7.5: Optimizing Audio for Various Platforms

When developing a game using CryEngine, it's crucial to optimize audio for various platforms to ensure that your game runs smoothly and delivers a consistent audio experience across different devices. In this section, we will discuss strategies and techniques for optimizing audio in CryEngine for a wide range of platforms.

Platform-Specific Audio Settings

Different gaming platforms, such as PC, consoles, and mobile devices, have varying hardware capabilities and performance constraints. To optimize audio, it's essential to customize audio settings for each target platform. CryEngine provides platform-specific settings that allow you to adjust audio quality and performance options accordingly.

Audio Compression

Audio files can be quite large, especially in high-quality formats like WAV or FLAC. To reduce file size and improve loading times, consider compressing audio assets using industry-standard audio codecs like AAC, MP3, or Ogg Vorbis. However, be mindful of the trade-off between compression and audio quality, as excessive compression may result in noticeable degradation.

```
-- Example of specifying audio compression settings in CryEngine
Audio.SetCompressionFormat("mobile_platform", "aac")
```

Audio Streaming

For open-world or large-scale games, streaming audio data from storage rather than loading it entirely into memory can be more memory-efficient. CryEngine supports streaming audio assets, allowing you to load and play audio dynamically as needed, reducing memory usage and improving performance.

```
-- Example of setting up audio streaming in CryEngine
Audio.SetStreamingEnabled(true)
```

LOD (Level of Detail) for Audio

Implementing audio LOD is similar to visual LOD. You can reduce the audio quality or complexity of sounds when they are farther away from the player, thus conserving resources. This ensures that audio processing remains efficient even in expansive game worlds.

Runtime Audio Asset Management

Manage audio assets efficiently during runtime by unloading and loading them as necessary. For example, you can unload audio assets associated with a specific game level or area once the player progresses to a different part of the game. This practice helps keep memory usage in check.

```
-- Example of unloading audio assets during gameplay
Audio.UnloadAssets("level_1_assets")
```

Profiling and Optimization Tools

CryEngine provides profiling and optimization tools to help you identify performance bottlenecks related to audio. Use these tools to monitor audio-related metrics, such as CPU usage, memory consumption, and streaming performance. Optimizing audio assets and logic based on these insights can lead to better overall performance.

Cross-Platform Compatibility

If you plan to release your game on multiple platforms, ensure that audio assets and settings are compatible across all of them. Consistency in audio quality and behavior is essential to provide a unified gaming experience, regardless of the platform players use.

Lastly, involve players in the testing phase to gather feedback on audio quality and performance. Player feedback can uncover issues related to audio optimization that may have gone unnoticed during development. Addressing player concerns and optimizing audio accordingly can significantly enhance the overall gaming experience.

In conclusion, optimizing audio for various platforms in CryEngine is a critical step in ensuring your game runs smoothly and delivers an enjoyable auditory experience. By tailoring audio settings, implementing compression, streaming, LOD, and runtime management, as well as utilizing profiling tools and considering player feedback, you can achieve optimal audio performance across a wide range of gaming devices.

Chapter 8: AI and Machine Learning Integration

Section 8.1: Advanced AI Strategies for Game Logic

In the realm of game development, artificial intelligence (AI) plays a pivotal role in enhancing player experiences. From creating intelligent non-player characters (NPCs) to implementing sophisticated game mechanics, mastering AI is crucial for game developers. In this section, we will delve into advanced AI strategies for game logic in CryEngine.

Understanding AI Behavior Trees

AI behavior trees are hierarchical structures that dictate the decision-making process of NPCs in your game. Each node in the tree represents a specific behavior or action. Advanced AI strategies involve designing complex behavior trees that allow NPCs to react dynamically to the game world and player interactions.

```
<!-- Example of an AI behavior tree in CryEngine -->
<BehaviorTree>
    <Sequence>
        <MoveToLocation target="Player" />
        <Selector>
            <Attack target="Player" />
            <FleeFromEnemy />
        </Selector>
    </Sequence>
</BehaviorTree>
```

Reactive and Proactive AI

Reactive AI focuses on immediate responses to stimuli. In contrast, proactive AI anticipates player actions and plans ahead. Combining both approaches can create engaging and challenging AI opponents. Reactive AI can handle unexpected player behavior, while proactive AI can provide a more human-like experience by making predictions.

```
-- Example of a reactive AI script in CryEngine
function OnPlayerDetected()
    if IsPlayerInSight() then
        AttackPlayer()
    else
        SearchForPlayer()
    end
end
```

Learning and Adaptation

Advanced AI can learn from player behavior and adapt over time. Machine learning techniques, such as reinforcement learning or neural networks, can be employed to make NPCs more intelligent. They can optimize their strategies, learn from mistakes, and become more challenging adversaries.

```python
# Example of a reinforcement learning algorithm for AI in CryEngine
def QLearning():
    while not convergence():
        state = chooseState()
        action = chooseAction(state)
        reward = performActionAndGetReward(state, action)
        updateQValue(state, action, reward)
```

Navigation and Pathfinding

Efficient navigation is crucial for AI-controlled characters. Advanced pathfinding algorithms like A* (A-star) can help NPCs navigate complex environments. Implementing dynamic obstacle avoidance and crowd simulation can further enhance the realism of AI movement.

```cpp
// Example of A* pathfinding in CryEngine
Pathfinder::FindPath(startPosition, targetPosition);
```

Emotional AI

To create more immersive gaming experiences, consider implementing emotional AI. NPCs with emotions can express fear, anger, happiness, and more, influencing their decisions and interactions with the player. Emotional AI adds depth to storytelling and character development.

```lua
-- Example of emotional AI states in CryEngine
function OnPlayerApproach()
    if IsPlayerArmed() then
        SetEmotion("Fear")
    else
        SetEmotion("Friendliness")
    end
end
```

Testing and Iteration

Iterative testing and refinement are essential when implementing advanced AI strategies. Conduct playtesting sessions to assess AI behavior and adjust parameters as needed. Player feedback is invaluable in fine-tuning AI to ensure it enhances the overall gaming experience.

In conclusion, advanced AI strategies in CryEngine can elevate your game to new heights by creating intelligent, adaptive, and engaging NPCs. By mastering AI behavior trees, employing both reactive and proactive AI approaches, incorporating learning and adaptation, optimizing navigation and pathfinding, introducing emotional AI, and conducting rigorous testing, you can develop AI systems that captivate players and immerse them in your game world.

Section 8.2: Machine Learning Applications in CryEngine

Machine learning (ML) has gained prominence in the field of game development, revolutionizing how games are created and experienced. In this section, we will explore various machine learning applications in CryEngine and how they can enhance gameplay, graphics, and overall player engagement.

Training AI with Reinforcement Learning

Reinforcement learning is a powerful ML technique for training AI agents in CryEngine. By using reward-based systems, AI can learn to make optimal decisions and adapt to changing game scenarios. This is particularly useful for creating NPCs that exhibit lifelike behaviors and adapt to player actions.

```
# Example of reinforcement learning in CryEngine
def ReinforcementLearning():
    while not convergence():
        state = observeGame()
        action = chooseAction(state)
        reward = performActionAndGetReward(action)
        updatePolicy(state, action, reward)
```

Procedural Content Generation

ML algorithms can be employed to generate procedural game content, such as terrain, levels, and assets. By training models on existing content and allowing them to generate new variations, game developers can save time and resources while providing players with endless gameplay possibilities.

```
// Example of procedural terrain generation using ML in CryEngine
ProceduralTerrainGenerator generator;
Terrain terrain = generator.generateTerrain();
terrain.render();
```

Realistic Natural Language Processing (NLP)

Incorporating NLP into game dialogue and interactions can make conversations with NPCs more dynamic and immersive. ML models can analyze and generate natural language responses based on player input, allowing for more meaningful interactions and branching dialogues.

```
-- Example of NLP-driven dialogue system in CryEngine
function OnPlayerInteract()
    playerInput = getPlayerInput()
    response = generateResponse(playerInput)
    displayResponse(response)
end
```

Gesture and Voice Recognition

ML algorithms can enable gesture and voice recognition in CryEngine, enhancing player input options. Players can use hand gestures or voice commands to control characters, cast spells, or trigger in-game actions, providing a more immersive and intuitive gaming experience.

```
// Example of gesture recognition in CryEngine using ML
GestureRecognizer gestureRecognizer = new GestureRecognizer();
gestureRecognizer.LoadGestures("spells.gestures");
if (gestureRecognizer.Recognize(playerGesture) == "Fireball")
{
    castFireballSpell();
}
```

Player Behavior Analysis

ML can be used to analyze player behavior and preferences. By collecting and analyzing player data, developers can tailor in-game experiences, recommend content, and personalize gameplay to keep players engaged and satisfied.

```
# Example of player behavior analysis in CryEngine
def AnalyzePlayerBehavior():
    playerData = collectPlayerData()
    preferences = analyzePreferences(playerData)
    personalizeGameplay(preferences)
```

AI-Driven Dynamic Difficulty Adjustment

ML-powered dynamic difficulty adjustment (DDA) systems can adapt the game's difficulty based on the player's skill level and performance. This ensures that both novice and experienced players have a challenging and enjoyable experience.

```
// Example of AI-driven DDA in CryEngine
DifficultyAdjustmentSystem.adjustDifficulty(playerSkillLevel);
```

Testing and Optimization

Machine learning models in CryEngine require thorough testing and optimization to ensure they perform as intended. This includes testing AI behaviors, model accuracy, and performance impact. It's essential to fine-tune ML algorithms and parameters for optimal results.

In conclusion, machine learning applications in CryEngine offer exciting opportunities to enhance game development and player experiences. By leveraging ML techniques for AI training, procedural content generation, NLP, gesture and voice recognition, player behavior analysis, dynamic difficulty adjustment, and rigorous testing, developers can create more immersive, adaptive, and engaging games. As ML continues to evolve, its role in game development is likely to expand, leading to even more innovative and captivating gaming experiences.

Section 8.3: Creating Adaptive and Learning NPCs

Creating non-player characters (NPCs) that exhibit intelligent and adaptive behavior is a crucial aspect of modern game development. In this section, we will delve into the concept of adaptive and learning NPCs in CryEngine, exploring techniques to make in-game characters more dynamic and responsive to player actions.

Traditional vs. Adaptive NPCs

Traditionally, NPCs in games follow predefined scripts and behaviors, making them predictable to some extent. However, the gaming industry is moving towards adaptive NPCs that can learn from player interactions and adjust their behavior accordingly. This creates a more immersive and challenging gaming experience.

```
-- Traditional NPC behavior in CryEngine
function TraditionalNPCBehavior()
    while not playerNearby() do
        patrol()
    end
    engagePlayer()
    followScriptedActions()
end
```

Machine Learning for NPC Behavior

One approach to creating adaptive NPCs is to employ machine learning algorithms. These algorithms can be trained on player data to understand different playstyles and adapt NPC behavior to match them. For example, an NPC might learn to employ different combat tactics based on whether the player prefers stealth or direct confrontation.

```
# Machine Learning for adaptive NPC behavior in CryEngine
def LearnFromPlayerData():
    playerData = collectPlayerData()
    adaptNPCBehavior(playerData)
```

Reinforcement Learning for NPCs

Reinforcement learning (RL) can be used to train NPCs to make decisions based on rewards and penalties. By defining a reward system, NPCs can learn which actions are beneficial and which are detrimental. For instance, an NPC can learn to avoid certain traps or seek cover during a firefight.

```
// Reinforcement Learning for NPCs in CryEngine
ReinforcementLearningAgent agent;
while (gameInProgress()) {
    state = observeEnvironment();
    action = agent.chooseAction(state);
```

```
    reward = performActionAndGetReward(action);
    agent.updatePolicy(state, action, reward);
}
```

Player Behavior Analysis

Another approach is to analyze player behavior and adjust NPC behavior accordingly. By collecting data on how players interact with NPCs and the choices they make, developers can fine-tune NPC responses. For instance, if players tend to negotiate rather than fight, NPCs can become more open to negotiations.

```
-- Player behavior analysis for adaptive NPCs in CryEngine
function AnalyzePlayerBehavior():
    playerData = collectPlayerData()
    adjustNPCResponses(playerData)
end
```

Dynamic Dialogues and Storylines

Adaptive NPCs can also impact the game's narrative. With machine learning and player data analysis, dialogues and storylines can evolve based on player choices and interactions. This creates a more personalized and immersive storytelling experience.

```
// Dynamic dialogues and storylines with adaptive NPCs in CryEngine
if (playerChoosesDiplomacy()) {
    dialogue = generateDiplomaticDialogue();
} else {
    dialogue = generateCombatDialogue();
}
```

Challenges and Considerations

While creating adaptive NPCs is exciting, it comes with challenges. Developers must balance the AI's adaptability with ensuring the game remains enjoyable and not frustrating for players. Additionally, rigorous testing and fine-tuning are essential to avoid unexpected and undesirable NPC behaviors.

In conclusion, the implementation of adaptive and learning NPCs in CryEngine represents a significant advancement in game development. Whether through machine learning, reinforcement learning, player behavior analysis, or dynamic storytelling, these NPCs offer a more immersive and responsive gaming experience. As technology continues to evolve, adaptive NPCs are likely to become even more integral to the future of game design.

Section 8.4: AI Challenges: Balancing and Fair Play

Implementing AI in games poses unique challenges related to maintaining game balance and ensuring fair play. In this section, we will explore the complexities involved in achieving balance between player and AI interactions while keeping the gaming experience enjoyable and challenging.

Balancing Act

Balancing AI is a critical aspect of game design. If AI opponents are too easy, players may become bored; if they are too difficult, players may become frustrated. Striking the right balance is essential to keep players engaged.

```
-- Balancing AI difficulty in CryEngine
function BalanceAI():
    adjustAIStats()
    playtestExtensively()
end
```

Adaptive Difficulty

One approach to balancing AI is to implement adaptive difficulty systems. These systems assess the player's performance and adjust the AI's skill level accordingly. If a player is struggling, the AI becomes more forgiving, and if a player is excelling, the AI presents a greater challenge.

```
// Adaptive difficulty for AI in CryEngine
void AdjustAIDifficulty() {
    playerPerformance = measurePlayerSkills();
    if (playerPerformance < threshold) {
        increaseAIDifficulty();
    } else if (playerPerformance > threshold) {
        decreaseAIDifficulty();
    }
}
```

Fair Play and Transparency

Maintaining fair play is crucial to the player experience. AI should not rely on unfair advantages, such as omniscience or unlimited resources. Transparent AI behavior, where players can understand why AI makes certain decisions, is key to ensuring fairness.

```
# Fair play and transparency in AI behavior
def EnsureFairPlay():
    if AIUsesSpecialAbilities():
        explainAIAbilities()
    if AIPerformsUnusualActions():
        provideReasoning()
```

AI Versatility

AI should be versatile and capable of adapting to different player strategies. This prevents players from exploiting predictable AI patterns and encourages diverse gameplay.

```
// Versatile AI behavior in CryEngine
void AdaptToPlayerStrategies() {
    if (playerPrefersStealth()) {
        adaptAIForStealth();
    } else if (playerPrefersCombat()) {
        adaptAIForCombat();
    }
}
```

Playtesting and Feedback

Continuous playtesting and player feedback are essential for balancing AI. Developers must iterate on AI behavior based on player experiences and suggestions to fine-tune the gaming experience.

```
// Playtesting and feedback for AI in CryEngine
if (playerReportsAIUnfairness()) {
    adjustAIParameters();
    gatherAdditionalFeedback();
}
```

Challenges in Multiplayer Games

Balancing AI becomes even more complex in multiplayer games, where AI must be challenging but not overpowered. In such cases, AI should complement player experiences rather than dominate them.

Conclusion

Balancing AI in games is an ongoing process that requires a deep understanding of player behavior and iterative adjustments to AI behavior. Striking the right balance between challenge and fairness is essential to create enjoyable and immersive gaming experiences. With the continued advancement of AI technologies, game developers have a wealth of tools and techniques at their disposal to enhance AI interactions while maintaining the integrity of the gameplay.

Section 8.5: AI Challenges: Balancing and Fair Play

AI challenges related to balancing and ensuring fair play are fundamental aspects of game development. In this section, we will delve deeper into the intricate balance that developers must strike to create an engaging and equitable gaming experience.

Balancing Act

Balancing AI is an art that requires careful consideration. Developers must find the sweet spot where AI opponents are neither too easy nor too difficult, ensuring that players are consistently engaged.

```
-- Balancing AI Difficulty in CryEngine
function BalanceAI():
    AdjustAIStats()
    PlaytestExtensively()
end
```

Adaptive Difficulty

Adaptive difficulty systems are a valuable tool in balancing AI. These systems assess the player's performance and dynamically adjust the AI's skill level to maintain an appropriate challenge level.

```
// Implementing Adaptive Difficulty for AI in CryEngine
void AdjustAIDifficulty() {
    playerPerformance = MeasurePlayerSkills();
    if (playerPerformance < threshold) {
        IncreaseAIDifficulty();
    } else if (playerPerformance > threshold) {
        DecreaseAIDifficulty();
    }
}
```

Fair Play and Transparency

Ensuring fair play is paramount. AI should not possess unfair advantages, such as omniscience or infinite resources. Transparent AI behavior, where players can comprehend the reasoning behind AI decisions, is essential for fairness.

```
# Upholding Fair Play and Transparency in AI Behavior
def EnsureFairPlay():
    if AIUtilizesSpecialAbilities():
        ExplainAIAbilities()
    if AIPerformsUnusualActions():
        ProvideReasoning()
```

AI Versatility

AI should exhibit versatility, capable of adapting to various player strategies. This prevents players from exploiting predictable AI patterns and encourages diverse gameplay experiences.

```
// Implementing Versatile AI Behavior in CryEngine
void AdaptToPlayerStrategies() {
    if (playerPrefersStealth()) {
        AdaptAIForStealth();
    } else if (playerPrefersCombat()) {
        AdaptAIForCombat();
    }
}
```

Playtesting and Feedback

Continuous playtesting and gathering player feedback are essential for refining AI balance. Developers must iterate on AI behavior based on player experiences and suggestions to fine-tune the gaming experience.

```
// Incorporating Playtesting and Feedback for AI in CryEngine
if (playerReportsAIUnfairness()) {
    AdjustAIParameters();
    GatherAdditionalFeedback();
}
```

Challenges in Multiplayer Games

Balancing AI in multiplayer games adds complexity as AI must be challenging but not overpowering. In such scenarios, AI should complement player experiences rather than dominate them.

Conclusion

Balancing AI in games is a perpetual journey that demands a profound comprehension of player behavior and continuous adjustments to AI behavior. Striking the right equilibrium between challenge and fairness is the key to creating enjoyable and immersive gaming experiences. With the constant evolution of AI technologies, game developers have a rich array of tools and techniques at their disposal to elevate AI interactions while preserving the integrity of gameplay.

Chapter 9: Networked and Multiplayer Game Development

Section 9.1: Advanced Networking and Multiplayer Systems

In this section, we will explore the intricate world of advanced networking and multiplayer systems in game development. Creating robust online multiplayer experiences is a complex task that involves various challenges and considerations.

Networking Fundamentals

Networked games rely on the transmission of data between players and servers. Understanding the fundamentals of networking protocols, latency, and data synchronization is crucial.

```
// Basic Network Packet Transmission
void SendPacket(Packet packet, Player recipient) {
    if (IsConnectedToServer()) {
        TransmitPacket(packet, recipient);
    }
}
```

Server-Client Architecture

Most multiplayer games use a client-server architecture. The server acts as the authoritative source of game state, while clients send their inputs to the server for validation.

```
// Server-Client Interaction in CryEngine
void ReceiveClientInput(Input input, Client client) {
    ValidateInput(input);
    UpdateGameWorld();
    SynchronizeGameState(client);
}
```

Latency Compensation

Dealing with latency is a challenge. Latency compensation techniques, such as client-side prediction and server reconciliation, ensure smooth gameplay despite network delays.

```
# Latency Compensation with Client-Side Prediction
def PredictClientMovement():
    if InputReceived():
        SimulateClientMovement()
        SendInputToServer()
    ReceiveServerUpdates()
    UpdateClientGameState()
```

Scalability and Load Balancing

As player numbers increase, games must scale to accommodate the load. Load balancing distributes players across multiple server instances to maintain performance.

```
// Load Balancing Strategies for Multiplayer Games
function DistributePlayersToServers(players) {
    const servers = FindAvailableServers();
    BalancePlayerDistribution(players, servers);
}
```

Security Measures

Security is paramount in multiplayer games. Developers implement measures like encryption, authentication, and server-side validation to prevent cheating and unauthorized access.

```
// Implementing Security Measures in Multiplayer Games
void EncryptAndValidateData(Packet data) {
    if (IsDataValid(data)) {
        DecryptAndProcess(data);
    }
}
```

Cross-Platform Multiplayer

Cross-platform multiplayer enables players on different devices to play together. Achieving compatibility and ensuring fairness is a complex task.

```
// Enabling Cross-Platform Multiplayer in CryEngine
void EnableCrossPlatformPlay() {
    if (IsCrossPlatformMatch()) {
        ApplyBalancingRules();
        SynchronizeGameState();
    }
}
```

Player Progression and Persistence

In multiplayer games, player progression and persistence are crucial. Implementing systems for character progression, achievements, and persistent worlds enhances player engagement.

```
-- Managing Player Progression in Multiplayer Games
function TrackPlayerAchievements(player, achievement) {
    player.TrackAchievementProgress(achievement);
    PersistAchievements(player);
}
```

Conclusion

Creating compelling networked and multiplayer games requires a deep understanding of networking concepts, server-client interactions, latency mitigation, scalability, security, and cross-platform compatibility. Game developers must continuously refine their multiplayer systems to provide players with immersive and enjoyable online experiences. By mastering these advanced networking and multiplayer techniques, developers can unlock new possibilities for multiplayer gaming across various platforms.

Section 9.2: Creating Robust Online Multiplayer Experiences

In this section, we delve into the process of creating robust online multiplayer experiences that captivate players and keep them engaged for hours on end. Robust multiplayer experiences are built on a foundation of reliable networking, intuitive gameplay, and community engagement.

Seamless Matchmaking

Matchmaking is the backbone of online multiplayer games. It connects players of similar skill levels and preferences, ensuring balanced and enjoyable matches.

```
# Matchmaking Algorithm
def Matchmake(players):
    for player in players:
        match = FindMatch(player)
        StartMatch(match)
```

Player Progression and Rewards

Implementing player progression systems with rewards, achievements, and leaderboards adds depth and motivation to multiplayer gameplay.

```
// Player Progression System
function RewardPlayer(player, experiencePoints) {
    player.GainExperience(experiencePoints);
    player.CheckAchievements();
    UpdateLeaderboards();
}
```

Social Features

Social features like friend lists, chat, and party systems foster a sense of community among players and encourage them to invite friends to the game.

```
// Building Social Features
void InviteFriend(Player player, Friend friend) {
    player.AddFriend(friend);
```

```
    SendInvitation(player, friend);
}
```

Balancing and Fair Play

Maintaining balance and fair play in multiplayer games is critical to retaining player interest. Anti-cheat measures and skill-based matchmaking contribute to a level playing field.

```
-- Skill-Based Matchmaking
function MatchmakePlayers(players) {
    for player in players do
        match = FindMatchBySkill(player.skillRating)
        StartMatch(match)
    end
end
```

Live Operations and Events

Live operations, such as in-game events and limited-time offers, create a dynamic multiplayer environment that keeps players coming back for more.

```
// In-Game Event System
void StartEvent(Event event) {
    event.Activate();
    InformPlayers(event);
}
```

Server Maintenance and Updates

Regular server maintenance and updates are necessary to ensure stability and introduce new content or features. Effective communication with the player community during downtime is crucial.

```
# Server Maintenance Protocol
def PerformMaintenance(server):
    NotifyPlayers(server, "Server maintenance in progress...")
    UpdateServer(server)
    NotifyPlayers(server, "Maintenance complete. Enjoy the updates!")
```

Community Feedback and Engagement

Engaging with the player community through forums, social media, and surveys helps developers understand player preferences and make informed decisions about game updates.

```
// Collecting Player Feedback
function CollectPlayerFeedback(feedbackForm) {
    AnalyzeFeedback(feedbackForm);
    Incorporate Suggestions into Development
    Keep Players Informed of Upcoming Changes
}
```

Player Support and Reporting

Providing robust player support and reporting mechanisms allows players to resolve issues and report misconduct, enhancing the overall multiplayer experience.

```
// Player Support System
void ReportPlayerMisconduct(Player reporter, Player reportedPlayer) {
    HandleMisconductReport(reporter, reportedPlayer);
    Enforce Fair Play Rules
    Provide Feedback to Reporters
}
```

Conclusion

Creating robust online multiplayer experiences is a multifaceted endeavor that involves matchmaking, player progression, social features, fair play, live operations, server maintenance, community engagement, and player support. Game developers who excel in these areas can build thriving multiplayer communities and deliver memorable experiences that keep players returning to their games time and time again. By embracing the principles outlined in this section, developers can craft online multiplayer worlds that stand the test of time.

Section 9.3: Server Management and Scalability

In this section, we will explore the critical aspects of server management and scalability in the context of online multiplayer game development. Efficient server management is essential to ensure that your game runs smoothly and can accommodate a growing player base. Scalability is key to handling increased traffic and maintaining a positive player experience.

Server Architecture

The architecture of your game servers plays a pivotal role in determining their performance and scalability. You can choose between various server architectures, including:

- **Single-Server:** Suitable for small games or prototypes, where a single server handles all player connections. This approach lacks scalability and fault tolerance.

- **Distributed Servers:** In this architecture, multiple servers work together to handle player connections. Load balancers distribute incoming requests among these servers, ensuring better scalability and redundancy.

- **Server Clusters:** Clusters of servers that can scale horizontally to accommodate more players. This approach is highly scalable and resilient, but it requires a more complex setup.

Load Balancing

Load balancing is a crucial technique for distributing incoming player connections evenly across multiple servers. A load balancer acts as a traffic cop, directing players to the least busy server. Load balancing helps prevent server overload and ensures a smooth gameplay experience.

```
# Load Balancer Algorithm
def LoadBalance(serverList, player):
    selectedServer = SelectServerWithLowestLoad(serverList)
    ConnectPlayerToServer(player, selectedServer)
```

Dynamic Scaling

Dynamic scaling allows your game's server capacity to automatically adjust based on real-time traffic. Cloud-based solutions like AWS, Azure, and Google Cloud offer tools for dynamic scaling, ensuring that you have the resources you need during peak demand.

```
# Auto-scaling Configuration (AWS)
aws autoscaling create-auto-scaling-group --auto-scaling-group-name MyGameSer
verGroup --launch-configuration-name MyLaunchConfig --min-size 2 --max-size 1
0 --desired-capacity 4
```

Database Scalability

Besides server scalability, you should consider the scalability of your game's database. Use techniques like database sharding, caching, and replication to ensure that your database can handle a growing player base and large volumes of data.

```
-- Sharding Example (SQL)
CREATE TABLE player_data (
    shard_key INT,
    player_id INT,
    data JSON
);
```

Monitoring and Analytics

Implement robust monitoring and analytics to gain insights into server performance and player behavior. Tools like Prometheus, Grafana, and Google Analytics can help you track server metrics, player engagement, and user retention.

```
# Prometheus Configuration
global:
  scrape_interval: 15s
scrape_configs:
  - job_name: 'game-server'
    static_configs:
      - targets: ['localhost:9090']
```

Disaster Recovery and Redundancy

Plan for disaster recovery by setting up redundant servers and databases. Regularly back up your game data and have a plan in place to quickly recover from server failures or data loss.

```bash
# Automated Backup Script
#!/bin/bash
backup_dir=/backup
timestamp=$(date +"%Y%m%d%H%M%S")
backup_file="$backup_dir/backup_$timestamp.tar.gz"
tar -czvf $backup_file /game_data
```

Player Data Security

Protect player data by implementing encryption, access controls, and security best practices. Ensure that sensitive player information is stored securely and that data breaches are minimized.

```python
# Player Data Encryption
def EncryptPlayerData(data):
    encrypted_data = encrypt(data, encryption_key)
    return encrypted_data
```

Conclusion

Server management and scalability are pivotal to the success of online multiplayer games. Whether you're developing a small indie game or a large-scale MMO, understanding server architecture, load balancing, dynamic scaling, database scalability, monitoring, disaster recovery, data security, and redundancy is essential. By addressing these aspects, you can create a resilient and scalable infrastructure that can support your game's growth and provide players with a reliable and enjoyable online experience.

Section 9.4: Security Considerations in Online Gaming

In the world of online gaming, security is a paramount concern. Players invest time and often money into their gaming experiences, making it essential to protect their accounts, data, and overall gameplay. This section delves into the various security considerations that game developers must address to ensure a safe and enjoyable gaming environment.

Player Authentication

Player authentication is the first line of defense against unauthorized access to player accounts. Implement strong authentication methods, including:

- **Username and Password:** Encourage players to use unique, strong passwords. Implement password hashing and salting to protect stored passwords.

```python
# Password Hashing (Python)
import hashlib

def hash_password(password, salt):
    hashed_password = hashlib.sha256((password + salt).encode()).hexdigest()
    return hashed_password
```

- **Two-Factor Authentication (2FA):** Offer 2FA as an additional security layer. Popular methods include SMS-based codes, authentication apps, and email verification.

Secure Communication

Ensure that all communication between players and your game servers is secure. Use encryption protocols like SSL/TLS to protect data in transit. Protect sensitive data such as login credentials, payment information, and player chat.

```javascript
// HTTPS Communication (Node.js)
const https = require('https');

const options = {
    hostname: 'api.example.com',
    port: 443,
    path: '/player/profile',
    method: 'GET'
};

const req = https.request(options, (res) => {
    // Handle response
});
```

Cheat Detection and Prevention

Combat cheating and hacking to maintain a fair gaming environment. Implement cheat detection algorithms and regularly update them to identify and punish cheaters. Consider using machine learning models to detect suspicious behavior patterns.

```python
# Cheat Detection (Python)
def detect_cheating(player_data):
    if suspicious_patterns_detected(player_data):
        ban_player(player_data)
```

Data Encryption

Encrypt sensitive player data, including payment information and personal details, both at rest and in transit. Use industry-standard encryption algorithms and keep encryption keys secure.

```java
// Data Encryption (Java)
import javax.crypto.Cipher;
import javax.crypto.KeyGenerator;
```

```java
import javax.crypto.SecretKey;

KeyGenerator keyGen = KeyGenerator.getInstance("AES");
keyGen.init(256);
SecretKey secretKey = keyGen.generateKey();

Cipher cipher = Cipher.getInstance("AES");
cipher.init(Cipher.ENCRYPT_MODE, secretKey);
byte[] encryptedData = cipher.doFinal(playerSensitiveData);
```

Regular Security Audits

Perform regular security audits and penetration testing to identify vulnerabilities in your game's infrastructure. Address any issues promptly and keep your game server software and libraries up-to-date to mitigate security risks.

```
# Penetration Testing (Command Line)
nmap -sV -p 1-65535 -T4 -A -v api.example.com
```

User Reporting and Moderation

Allow players to report suspicious behavior or offensive content. Implement moderation tools to review and take action against reported issues promptly. Enforce community guidelines and policies.

```javascript
// User Reporting (JavaScript)
function reportPlayer(playerID, reason) {
    // Send report to moderation team
}

function moderateContent(reportedContent) {
    // Review and take appropriate action
}
```

Legal and Compliance

Stay informed about legal requirements and regulations related to online gaming, especially regarding player data protection, age restrictions, and compliance with regional laws. Consult legal experts if necessary.

Conclusion

Security is a shared responsibility between game developers and players. By implementing robust security measures, ensuring secure authentication and communication, addressing cheat detection, encrypting sensitive data, conducting regular security audits, enabling user reporting and moderation, and staying compliant with relevant laws, game developers can create a safer and more enjoyable online gaming environment. Player trust and the integrity of the gaming experience are vital for the long-term success of online games.

Section 9.5: Implementing Cross-Platform Multiplayer Features

Cross-platform multiplayer gaming has become increasingly popular, allowing players on different devices and platforms to play together. Implementing cross-platform multiplayer features can enhance the player base and provide a more inclusive gaming experience. In this section, we will explore the challenges and best practices for enabling cross-platform multiplayer gaming in your online game.

Challenges in Cross-Platform Multiplayer

Enabling cross-platform multiplayer gaming presents several challenges that developers need to address:

1. **Platform Disparities:** Different platforms may have varying performance capabilities, input methods, and control schemes. Balancing gameplay to ensure fairness can be challenging.

2. **Cross-Network Play:** Integrating different network infrastructures, including those on consoles, PC, and mobile, can be complex. You must ensure seamless connectivity between players.

3. **User Interface (UI):** Designing a UI that accommodates various screen sizes and input methods while maintaining a consistent user experience is essential.

4. **Regulatory and Policy Compliance:** Each platform may have its own policies and regulations, which can affect gameplay and content. Developers must navigate these requirements.

5. **Content Synchronization:** Keeping game content and updates synchronized across platforms, especially when new content is released, can be tricky.

Best Practices for Cross-Platform Multiplayer

To successfully implement cross-platform multiplayer features, consider the following best practices:

1. **Balanced Gameplay:** Implement a robust matchmaking system that considers players' skills and the platform they are playing on. This helps maintain balanced gameplay.

2. **Input Compatibility:** Ensure that the game supports various input methods, including game controllers, keyboard and mouse, and touch controls. Players should feel comfortable playing on their chosen platform.

3. **Cross-Progression:** Allow players to carry their progress, achievements, and items across platforms. This encourages player loyalty and engagement.

4. **Unified Player IDs:** Use a unified player ID system to identify players across different platforms. This simplifies friend requests, leaderboards, and in-game interactions.

5. **Cross-Network Play:** Collaborate with platform providers to enable cross-network play. Platforms like Xbox Live and PlayStation Network offer such capabilities.

6. **Testing and Feedback:** Conduct thorough testing on different platforms and gather feedback from players to identify and address platform-specific issues.

7. **Community Building:** Encourage cross-platform multiplayer by fostering a strong gaming community that promotes inclusivity and fun. Host cross-platform events and tournaments.

8. **Content Rollouts:** Plan content updates and releases carefully to ensure simultaneous availability across all platforms. This prevents fragmentation of the player base.

Code Implementation (Unified Player ID)

Here's a simplified code example in Python for implementing a unified player ID system:

```python
class Player:
    def __init__(self, username, platform):
        self.username = username
        self.platform = platform
        self.player_id = self.generate_player_id()

    def generate_player_id(self):
        # Generate a unique player ID based on username and platform
        return f"{self.username}_{self.platform}"

# Example usage
player1 = Player("JohnDoe", "PC")
player2 = Player("JaneSmith", "Xbox")

print(player1.player_id)  # Output: JohnDoe_PC
print(player2.player_id)  # Output: JaneSmith_Xbox
```

Conclusion

Implementing cross-platform multiplayer features can be challenging but highly rewarding for game developers. By addressing platform disparities, ensuring input compatibility, supporting cross-progression, using unified player IDs, enabling cross-network play, conducting thorough testing, fostering a strong community, and planning content rollouts carefully, developers can create a more inclusive and enjoyable gaming experience for players across various platforms. Cross-platform multiplayer gaming is a significant step toward expanding your game's reach and player base.

123

Chapter 10: Interface Design and User Experience

Section 10.1: Creating Intuitive and Customizable UIs

User interface (UI) design is a critical aspect of game development, directly impacting the user experience (UX). In this section, we will delve into the principles and techniques for creating intuitive and customizable UIs that enhance gameplay and engage players effectively.

Importance of UI in Game Design

UI elements, including menus, buttons, HUDs (Heads-Up Displays), and interactive components, serve as the player's bridge to the game world. A well-designed UI can make the difference between a frustrating or immersive gaming experience.

Principles of UI Design

1. *Clarity and Simplicity: Keep the UI simple and straightforward. Avoid clutter and excessive information. Use clear icons and labels.*

2. *Consistency: Maintain a consistent visual style throughout the game. Ensure that UI elements, fonts, and colors match the game's theme.*

3. *User-Friendly Navigation: Make it easy for players to navigate menus and options. Provide intuitive pathways to different sections.*

4. *Feedback and Response: UI elements should respond promptly to player actions. Provide visual and auditory feedback to confirm actions.*

5. *Customization: Allow players to customize the UI to their preferences. Options for resizing, repositioning, or hiding UI elements can improve accessibility.*

6. *Accessibility: Ensure that the UI is accessible to players with disabilities. Use accessible colors, provide keyboard shortcuts, and offer screen reader support.*

Designing Intuitive UIs

Creating intuitive UIs requires an understanding of player expectations and behaviors. Here are some tips:

- **Player-Centered Design:** Consider player feedback and preferences during UI development. Conduct user testing to identify pain points.

- **Visual Hierarchy:** Prioritize important information and actions by using size, color, and placement. Guide the player's attention effectively.

- **Minimalism:** Avoid unnecessary elements that may overwhelm players. Present only what is essential for gameplay.

124

- **Progressive Disclosure:** Introduce complex options gradually, especially in tutorial sequences. Avoid overwhelming new players with too much information.

Code Implementation (UI Button)

Here's a simple code example in C# for creating a UI button in Unity:

```csharp
using UnityEngine;
using UnityEngine.UI;

public class UIButton : MonoBehaviour
{
    public Text buttonText;

    private void Start()
    {
        // Add a Listener to the button's click event
        Button button = GetComponent<Button>();
        button.onClick.AddListener(HandleButtonClick);
    }

    private void HandleButtonClick()
    {
        // Handle the button click event
        buttonText.text = "Clicked!";
    }
}
```

Customizable UIs

Customizable UIs empower players to tailor their gaming experience. Here are some customizable UI features to consider:

- **Key Binding:** Allow players to rebind keys and controls according to their preferences.

- **HUD Elements:** Permit players to move, resize, or hide HUD elements like health bars, minimaps, or quest trackers.

- **UI Themes:** Offer different visual themes or skins that players can choose from.

- **Accessibility Settings:** Provide options for adjusting text size, contrast, and color schemes.

Conclusion

Creating intuitive and customizable UIs is essential for delivering an enjoyable gaming experience. By adhering to UI design principles, understanding player behavior, and implementing customization options, developers can enhance the accessibility, usability, and overall quality of their games. A well-crafted UI not only facilitates gameplay but also immerses players in the game world, making it a fundamental aspect of game design and user experience.

Section 10.2: Advanced HUD and Interface Elements

In this section, we will explore advanced HUD (Heads-Up Display) and interface elements that can elevate the user interface (UI) design of your game. HUD elements play a crucial role in providing players with essential information during gameplay, and creating a well-crafted HUD contributes significantly to the overall user experience.

Dynamic HUD Elements

One way to enhance your game's HUD is to make elements dynamic and context-sensitive. Rather than cluttering the screen with permanent indicators, you can display relevant information only when necessary. For example:

- **Health Bars:** Show health bars above characters during combat, but hide them during exploration or dialogue scenes.

- **Objective Markers:** Display objective markers when a quest is active and hide them when not needed.

- **Ammo Count:** Show the player's remaining ammo only when they are using a weapon or item that requires it.

Dynamic HUD elements reduce visual clutter, keep the player focused on the game world, and provide information precisely when it's relevant.

Interactive HUD Elements

Consider adding interactive elements to your HUD. These elements allow players to directly interact with the UI to perform actions or access features. Examples include:

- **Quick Access Menus:** Allow players to open inventory, select weapons, or use consumables through a quick-access menu on the HUD.

- **Map Interaction:** Enable players to set waypoints, zoom in/out, or toggle map filters directly from the HUD map.

- **Quest Tracking:** Allow players to manage quests and objectives from the HUD, marking objectives as complete or setting active quests.

Interactive HUD elements streamline gameplay by reducing the need to navigate through complex menus, creating a more immersive experience.

Different gameplay situations may require varying HUD layouts. For instance, a first-person shooter may need a different HUD setup compared to a strategy game. Implement adaptive HUD layouts that adjust based on the game context:

- **Combat HUD:** When in combat, emphasize health, ammo, and weapon information, and minimize non-essential elements.

- **Exploration HUD:** In exploration or puzzle-solving scenarios, prioritize environmental details and objectives.

- **Dialogue HUD:** During dialogues or cutscenes, display character portraits and dialogue options prominently.

Adaptive HUD layouts ensure that players have the most relevant information at their fingertips, enhancing their gameplay experience.

Code Example (Unity - Dynamic HUD)

Here's a simplified Unity script in C# for creating a dynamic HUD element that displays player health when taking damage and hides it when health is full:

```csharp
using UnityEngine;
using UnityEngine.UI;

public class DynamicHealthHUD : MonoBehaviour
{
    public Text healthText;
    private PlayerHealth playerHealth;

    private void Start()
    {
        playerHealth = GetComponent<PlayerHealth>();
        UpdateHUD();

        // Subscribe to the OnHealthChanged event
        playerHealth.OnHealthChanged += UpdateHUD;
    }

    private void UpdateHUD()
    {
        healthText.text = "Health: " + playerHealth.CurrentHealth;

        // Hide the HUD if health is full
        if (playerHealth.CurrentHealth == playerHealth.MaxHealth)
        {
            healthText.gameObject.SetActive(false);
        }
        else
```

```
        {
            healthText.gameObject.SetActive(true);
        }
    }
}
```

Advanced HUD and interface elements can significantly enhance the user interface of your game. By making HUD elements dynamic and context-sensitive, adding interactivity, and implementing adaptive layouts, you can create a UI that not only provides essential information but also contributes to a more immersive and enjoyable gaming experience. Careful consideration of these elements can set your game apart and cater to the preferences of different players.

Section 10.3: Integrating UI with Gameplay and Story

In this section, we will explore the critical aspect of integrating your user interface (UI) with gameplay and storytelling in your game. UI is more than just a set of menus and HUD elements; it plays a vital role in conveying the game's narrative, guiding players, and enhancing immersion.

Narrative-Driven UI

Consider how your UI elements can contribute to your game's storytelling. UI can be used to deliver information in ways that align with the narrative, such as:

- **In-Game Documents:** Present lore, diaries, or letters as interactive in-game documents that players can find and read.

- **Character Journals:** Allow players to access character journals that provide insights into the protagonist's thoughts and experiences.

- **Environmental Clues:** Use UI elements to highlight important objects or areas in the environment, encouraging exploration and discovery.

By integrating UI with the narrative, you can immerse players further in your game's world and storytelling.

Dialogue and Choice Systems

Your game's dialogue and choice systems are core components of the player's interaction with the story. UI for dialogue should be designed to:

- **Emphasize Character Emotions:** Use character portraits, animations, and text effects to convey emotions during conversations.

- **Clear Choice Presentation:** Ensure dialogue choices are presented clearly, and the consequences of those choices are transparent.

- **Branching Narratives:** Design UI that accommodates branching storylines and player decisions, providing feedback on the consequences of their choices.

A well-designed dialogue and choice UI can make the storytelling experience more engaging and emotionally resonant.

Gameplay Feedback

UI elements can provide valuable feedback to players during gameplay. This feedback helps players understand their progress, objectives, and the consequences of their actions. Examples include:

- **Objective Updates:** Display clear objectives and progress indicators, so players always know what to do next.

- **Resource Management:** Show resource inventories, stamina bars, or ammunition counts to aid decision-making during gameplay.

- **Status Effects:** Use visual icons and tooltips to inform players of status effects like poison, buffs, or debuffs.

Effective gameplay feedback through UI prevents frustration and confusion, improving the overall player experience.

Code Example (Unity - Narrative-Driven UI)

Here's a simplified Unity script in C# for creating an in-game document UI that players can interact with to access narrative content:

```csharp
using UnityEngine;
using UnityEngine.UI;

public class InGameDocument : MonoBehaviour
{
    public GameObject documentUI;
    public Text documentText;
    public string documentContent;

    private bool isDocumentOpen = false;

    private void Start()
    {
        CloseDocument();
    }

    public void ToggleDocument()
    {
```

```
        if (isDocumentOpen)
        {
            CloseDocument();
        }
        else
        {
            OpenDocument();
        }
    }

    private void OpenDocument()
    {
        documentUI.SetActive(true);
        documentText.text = documentContent;
        isDocumentOpen = true;
    }

    private void CloseDocument()
    {
        documentUI.SetActive(false);
        documentText.text = string.Empty;
        isDocumentOpen = false;
    }
}
```

Conclusion

Integrating UI with gameplay and storytelling is a fundamental aspect of game design. Whether it's using UI elements to convey narrative, facilitate dialogue and choice systems, or provide gameplay feedback, a thoughtful approach to UI design can greatly enhance the player's immersion and engagement with your game. By considering how UI elements align with your game's narrative and gameplay, you can create a more cohesive and memorable gaming experience.

Section 10.4: Accessibility and Inclusive Design Practices

In this section, we'll delve into the essential topic of accessibility and inclusive design practices for user interfaces (UI) in game development. Ensuring that your game is accessible to a wide range of players, including those with disabilities, is not only an ethical responsibility but also a way to broaden your audience and create a more enjoyable gaming experience for everyone.

Understanding Accessibility

Accessibility in gaming refers to designing games and UI elements in a way that makes them usable by individuals with various disabilities. These disabilities may include visual, auditory, motor, cognitive, or neurological impairments. Here are some key principles to consider:

- **Perceivable:** Ensure that information and UI elements can be perceived through multiple sensory modalities. Provide alternatives for non-text content, such as images and audio.

- **Operable:** Make all interactive elements and controls operable using a variety of input methods, including keyboard, mouse, and gamepad. Avoid content that relies solely on timing or specific gestures.

- **Understandable:** Create clear and consistent navigation and UI structure. Use plain language and provide instructions and cues for users to understand how to interact with the game.

- **Robust:** Develop games that can withstand changes in technology and assistive technologies. This ensures that your game remains accessible as technology evolves.

Inclusive UI Design

Inclusive UI design focuses on creating interfaces that are welcoming to all players, regardless of their abilities. Here are some inclusive design practices to implement in your game's UI:

- **Customizable Controls:** Allow players to remap controls and adjust input sensitivity to accommodate their needs and preferences.

- **Text Size and Font Options:** Provide options to adjust text size and choose from different fonts for readability.

- **Colorblind-Friendly Palettes:** Use color schemes that are distinguishable for players with color vision deficiencies. Avoid conveying critical information solely through color.

- **Subtitles and Closed Captions:** Include subtitles and closed captions for dialogues and important audio cues. Allow players to customize caption size and placement.

- **Audio Cues and Visual Feedback:** Use a combination of audio cues and visual feedback to convey information. This helps players with hearing impairments and those who prefer to play with the sound off.

Testing with Diverse Audiences

To ensure the effectiveness of your accessibility and inclusive design efforts, it's crucial to test your game with a diverse group of players, including those with disabilities. Conduct usability testing and gather feedback to identify areas that may need improvement. Consider collaborating with accessibility experts or organizations focused on gaming accessibility.

Code Example (Unity - Customizable Controls)

Here's a simplified Unity script in C# that allows players to remap controls:

```csharp
using UnityEngine;
using UnityEngine.InputSystem;

public class CustomizableControls : MonoBehaviour
{
    public InputActionReference playerMovement;

    private void Awake()
    {
        // Load player's custom control bindings
        playerMovement.action.ApplyBindingOverride(
            "Vector2", PlayerPrefs.GetString("CustomMovementBinding", "Vector
2"));
    }

    // Function to allow players to customize controls
    public void RemapControls(string newBinding)
    {
        playerMovement.action.ApplyBindingOverride("Vector2", newBinding);
        PlayerPrefs.SetString("CustomMovementBinding", newBinding);
    }
}
```

Conclusion

Incorporating accessibility and inclusive design practices into your game's UI is a significant step toward creating a more welcoming and enjoyable gaming experience for all players. By understanding the principles of accessibility, implementing inclusive design features, and conducting thorough testing, you can ensure that your game is accessible to a diverse audience and reflects your commitment to inclusivity in game development.

Section 10.5: User Testing and Feedback Loops for UI/UX

User testing and feedback loops are integral components of user interface (UI) and user experience (UX) design in game development. In this section, we will explore the importance of conducting user testing, gathering feedback, and iterating on your game's UI/UX design to create a more enjoyable and player-friendly experience.

The Value of User Testing

User testing involves having real players interact with your game's UI and providing feedback on their experience. It is a crucial step in identifying usability issues, user preferences, and areas for improvement. Here are some key benefits of conducting user testing:

- **Identifying Pain Points:** User testing helps uncover pain points and frustrations that players may encounter while navigating your game's interface. This can include confusing menus, unclear instructions, or cumbersome controls.

- **Validation of Design Choices:** It validates whether your UI/UX design aligns with the expectations and needs of your target audience. Testing ensures that your design decisions resonate with real players.

- **Accessibility and Inclusivity:** User testing can reveal accessibility issues that may not be apparent during development. It allows you to make necessary adjustments to ensure your game is inclusive to all players.

- **Optimizing Flow:** By observing how players interact with your UI, you can identify areas where the user flow can be optimized for a smoother and more intuitive experience.

Setting Up User Tests

To conduct effective user testing, consider the following steps:

1. **Define Objectives:** Clearly define the goals and objectives of your user tests. What specific aspects of the UI/UX are you testing? What feedback are you seeking to gather?

2. **Recruit Participants:** Select a diverse group of participants that represent your target audience. Ensure that you include players with varying levels of experience.

3. **Create Test Scenarios:** Develop scenarios or tasks that participants will perform using your game's UI. These scenarios should align with your testing objectives.

4. **Moderated vs. Unmoderated Tests:** Decide whether you will conduct moderated tests, where a facilitator guides participants, or unmoderated tests, where participants interact with the game independently.

5. **Collect Data:** Gather data during the tests, including observations, player feedback, and metrics related to task completion and usability.

6. **Analyze and Iterate:** Analyze the collected data to identify issues and areas for improvement. Iterate on your UI/UX design based on the insights gained from user testing.

Feedback Loops and Continuous Improvement

User testing is not a one-time activity; it should be an ongoing part of your development process. Establish feedback loops where you regularly gather player feedback and make iterative improvements to your game's UI/UX. This continuous improvement approach ensures that your game stays aligned with player expectations and evolving design trends.

Code Example (Unity - Feedback Survey)

Here's a simplified Unity script in C# to prompt players for feedback through a survey:

```csharp
using UnityEngine;
using UnityEngine.UI;

public class FeedbackSurvey : MonoBehaviour
{
    public GameObject surveyPanel;
    public Text feedbackText;

    private void Start()
    {
        // Display the feedback survey panel
        surveyPanel.SetActive(true);
    }

    // Function to submit feedback
    public void SubmitFeedback()
    {
        string playerFeedback = feedbackText.text;
        // Send playerFeedback to your feedback collection system
        // ...
        // Close the survey panel
        surveyPanel.SetActive(false);
    }
}
```

Conclusion

User testing and feedback loops are vital components of creating a player-centric UI/UX in game development. By actively involving players in the testing process, gathering feedback, and continuously iterating on your design, you can enhance the usability and enjoyability of your game, ultimately leading to higher player satisfaction and engagement.

Chapter 11: Mobile Development with CryEngine

Section 11.1: Advanced Techniques for Mobile Game Development

Mobile game development has become a significant part of the gaming industry, with an ever-expanding audience of players on smartphones and tablets. In this section, we will explore advanced techniques for developing mobile games using CryEngine. These techniques will help you optimize your game for mobile platforms, create engaging touch-based interfaces, and leverage the unique features of mobile devices.

Developing high-performance games for mobile devices requires careful optimization. Here are some key considerations:

- **Graphics Optimization:** Mobile devices have varying levels of GPU capabilities. Implement efficient rendering techniques, reduce draw calls, and use level-of-detail (LOD) models to maintain a smooth frame rate.

- **Memory Management:** Mobile devices have limited memory. Implement memory management strategies, such as texture compression and asset streaming, to ensure your game runs smoothly without consuming excessive memory.

- **Battery Efficiency:** Optimize your game's power consumption to extend battery life. Minimize CPU and GPU usage when the device is not actively rendering frames.

Touch Interface and Controls

Mobile devices rely on touch-based controls, which provide unique opportunities for game design. Consider the following when designing touch interfaces:

- **Intuitive Gestures:** Utilize common touch gestures like tapping, swiping, pinching, and multi-touch to create intuitive and responsive controls.

- **On-Screen Buttons:** Design on-screen buttons and virtual joysticks that are large enough for touch input and provide tactile feedback.

- **Contextual Menus:** Implement context-sensitive menus that appear when players interact with specific objects or areas on the screen.

Mobile-Specific Features

Mobile devices offer several hardware features that can enhance gameplay and immersion:

- **Accelerometer and Gyroscope:** Use these sensors for motion-based controls or to create interactive gameplay elements.

- **Camera and GPS:** Incorporate the device's camera and GPS capabilities for augmented reality (AR) features or location-based gameplay.

- **Vibration and Haptic Feedback:** Provide tactile feedback to enhance the gaming experience and provide cues to players.

Cross-Platform Considerations

If you plan to release your game on multiple platforms, including mobile, consider these cross-platform development strategies:

- **Code Modularity:** Keep your game code modular and platform-independent, allowing for easier adaptation to different platforms.

- **UI Scalability:** Design your user interface to be scalable and adaptable to various screen sizes and resolutions.

- **Input Handling:** Implement a unified input handling system that can accommodate touch, keyboard, and controller inputs.

Code Example (Unity - Mobile Touch Input)

Here's a simplified Unity script in C# to handle touch input on mobile devices:

```csharp
using UnityEngine;

public class MobileTouchInput : MonoBehaviour
{
    private void Update()
    {
        // Check for touch input
        if (Input.touchCount > 0)
        {
            // Loop through all active touches
            foreach (Touch touch in Input.touches)
            {
                // Check for touch phase
                if (touch.phase == TouchPhase.Began)
                {
                    // Handle touch input, e.g., raycasting to interact with
objects
                    // ...
                }
            }
        }
    }
}
```

Conclusion

Developing mobile games with CryEngine requires a distinct set of skills and considerations compared to other platforms. By optimizing for performance, designing intuitive touch interfaces, leveraging mobile-specific features, and keeping cross-platform compatibility in mind, you can create successful and engaging mobile gaming experiences.

Chapter 11: Mobile Development with CryEngine

Section 11.1: Advanced Techniques for Mobile Game Development

Mobile game development has become a significant part of the gaming industry, with an ever-expanding audience of players on smartphones and tablets. In this section, we will explore advanced techniques for developing mobile games using CryEngine. These techniques will help you optimize your game for mobile platforms, create engaging touch-based interfaces, and leverage the unique features of mobile devices.

Optimizing for Mobile Performance

Developing high-performance games for mobile devices requires careful optimization. Here are some key considerations:

- **Graphics Optimization:** Mobile devices have varying levels of GPU capabilities. Implement efficient rendering techniques, reduce draw calls, and use level-of-detail (LOD) models to maintain a smooth frame rate.

- **Memory Management:** Mobile devices have limited memory. Implement memory management strategies, such as texture compression and asset streaming, to ensure your game runs smoothly without consuming excessive memory.

- **Battery Efficiency:** Optimize your game's power consumption to extend battery life. Minimize CPU and GPU usage when the device is not actively rendering frames.

Touch Interface and Controls

Mobile devices rely on touch-based controls, which provide unique opportunities for game design. Consider the following when designing touch interfaces:

- **Intuitive Gestures:** Utilize common touch gestures like tapping, swiping, pinching, and multi-touch to create intuitive and responsive controls.

- **On-Screen Buttons:** Design on-screen buttons and virtual joysticks that are large enough for touch input and provide tactile feedback.

- **Contextual Menus:** Implement context-sensitive menus that appear when players interact with specific objects or areas on the screen.

Mobile-Specific Features

Mobile devices offer several hardware features that can enhance gameplay and immersion:

- **Accelerometer and Gyroscope:** Use these sensors for motion-based controls or to create interactive gameplay elements.

- **Camera and GPS:** Incorporate the device's camera and GPS capabilities for augmented reality (AR) features or location-based gameplay.

- **Vibration and Haptic Feedback:** Provide tactile feedback to enhance the gaming experience and provide cues to players.

Cross-Platform Considerations

If you plan to release your game on multiple platforms, including mobile, consider these cross-platform development strategies:

- **Code Modularity:** Keep your game code modular and platform-independent, allowing for easier adaptation to different platforms.

- **UI Scalability:** Design your user interface to be scalable and adaptable to various screen sizes and resolutions.

- **Input Handling:** Implement a unified input handling system that can accommodate touch, keyboard, and controller inputs.

Code Example (Unity - Mobile Touch Input)

Here's a simplified Unity script in C# to handle touch input on mobile devices:

```csharp
using UnityEngine;

public class MobileTouchInput : MonoBehaviour
{
    private void Update()
    {
        // Check for touch input
        if (Input.touchCount > 0)
        {
            // Loop through all active touches
            foreach (Touch touch in Input.touches)
            {
                // Check for touch phase
                if (touch.phase == TouchPhase.Began)
                {
                    // Handle touch input, e.g., raycasting to interact with objects
                    // ...
                }
            }
        }
    }
}
```

Conclusion

Developing mobile games with CryEngine requires a distinct set of skills and considerations compared to other platforms. By optimizing for performance, designing intuitive touch interfaces, leveraging mobile-specific features, and keeping cross-platform compatibility in mind, you can create successful and engaging mobile gaming experiences.

Section 11.2: Optimizing CryEngine Games for Mobile Platforms

Optimizing CryEngine games for mobile platforms is crucial to ensure a smooth and enjoyable gaming experience on smartphones and tablets. While CryEngine is known for its high-quality graphics and advanced rendering capabilities, mobile devices have hardware limitations that require careful consideration. In this section, we will explore various strategies for optimizing CryEngine games to run efficiently on mobile platforms.

1. Asset Optimization:

- **Texture Compression:** Use texture compression formats suitable for mobile devices, such as ETC2 or ASTC, to reduce memory usage and improve loading times.

- **Model Simplification:** Create lower-poly versions of 3D models for mobile platforms to reduce GPU load and improve performance.

2. Level Design:

- **LOD (Level of Detail):** Implement LOD systems to dynamically reduce the detail of objects based on their distance from the camera, ensuring that distant objects have lower-poly versions.

- **Occlusion Culling:** Use occlusion culling techniques to avoid rendering objects that are not visible to the camera, further reducing GPU workload.

3. Graphics Settings:

- **Quality Settings:** Provide options for users to adjust graphics quality settings, allowing them to choose a balance between visual fidelity and performance.

- **Dynamic Resolution:** Implement dynamic resolution scaling to lower the rendering resolution during resource-intensive scenes, maintaining a smooth frame rate.

4. Lighting and Shading:

- **Mobile-Friendly Shaders:** Utilize shaders optimized for mobile platforms, avoiding complex shader effects that might be too demanding.

- **Real-Time Lighting:** Limit the number of dynamic lights and shadow-casting sources to improve performance, especially on older devices.

5. UI and Controls:

- **Touch Controls:** Design intuitive touch-based controls and user interfaces that are responsive and easy to use on touch screens.

- **UI Optimization:** Optimize UI elements and scripts to minimize CPU and GPU usage while rendering menus and HUD elements.

6. Audio Optimization:

- **Audio Compression:** Compress audio files to reduce memory usage and streaming overhead, considering different audio formats for mobile platforms.

- **Spatial Audio:** Use 3D audio techniques to enhance the immersive experience, but be mindful of the additional CPU cost.

7. Testing and Profiling:

- **Device Testing:** Test your game on a range of mobile devices with varying hardware specifications to ensure broad compatibility.

- **Profiling Tools:** Use profiling tools to identify performance bottlenecks and areas that require optimization.

8. Cross-Platform Development:

- **Code Reusability:** Maintain a shared codebase where possible to minimize the effort required to support multiple platforms, including mobile.

- **Platform-Specific Tweaks:** Implement platform-specific tweaks and settings to ensure optimal performance on each target platform.

Code Example (Unity - Dynamic Resolution Scaling):

Here's a simplified Unity C# script to implement dynamic resolution scaling based on the device's performance:

```csharp
using UnityEngine;

public class DynamicResolution : MonoBehaviour
{
    private void Start()
    {
        // Adjust the target frame rate for mobile devices
        Application.targetFrameRate = 30;

        // Determine the screen's original width and height
        float originalWidth = Screen.width;
        float originalHeight = Screen.height;

        // Calculate the desired resolution scale based on device performance
        float resolutionScale = DetermineResolutionScale();

        // Apply the resolution scale
        int scaledWidth = Mathf.FloorToInt(originalWidth * resolutionScale);
        int scaledHeight = Mathf.FloorToInt(originalHeight * resolutionScale)
;

        Screen.SetResolution(scaledWidth, scaledHeight, true);
    }
```

```
private float DetermineResolutionScale()
{
    // Implement logic to calculate the desired resolution scale based on
device performance
    // For example, consider CPU and GPU performance metrics.
    float performanceFactor = 0.5f; // Adjust this value based on your cr
iteria.
    return Mathf.Clamp01(performanceFactor);
}
}
```

Conclusion:

Optimizing CryEngine games for mobile platforms is a multi-faceted process that involves asset management, level design considerations, graphics settings, UI and control design, audio optimization, thorough testing, and cross-platform development strategies. By following these optimization techniques and considering the limitations of mobile hardware, you can create engaging and well-performing mobile games with CryEngine.

Section 11.3: Touch Interface and Mobile-Specific Features

When developing games for mobile platforms using CryEngine, it's essential to consider the touch interface and implement mobile-specific features to create a seamless and enjoyable gaming experience. Mobile devices rely on touch input, which differs significantly from traditional keyboard and mouse controls. In this section, we will explore best practices for designing touch-friendly interfaces and integrating mobile-specific features into your CryEngine games.

1. Touch Controls:

- **Intuitive Gestures:** Design intuitive touch gestures, such as swiping, tapping, pinching, and multi-finger gestures, to replace complex keyboard and mouse interactions.

- **Virtual Joysticks:** Implement virtual joysticks or thumbsticks for games that require analog control, such as movement or camera rotation.

- **Customizable Controls:** Provide players with options to customize the position and size of on-screen controls, catering to various device screen sizes and player preferences.

2. HUD and UI Design:

- **Responsive Layouts:** Create responsive user interfaces that adapt to different screen sizes and orientations, ensuring elements are appropriately spaced and legible.

- **Large Buttons:** Design larger touch-friendly buttons and icons to prevent accidental taps and improve usability on smaller screens.

- **Gesture-Based Menus:** Implement swipe-based menus or navigation systems that are more accessible and engaging for touch screens.

3. Mobile-Specific Features:

- **Accelerometer:** Utilize the device's accelerometer for gameplay mechanics, such as tilting the device to control in-game objects or vehicles.

- **Camera Integration:** Incorporate the device's camera for augmented reality (AR) features or interactive experiences.

- **GPS and Location Services:** Use GPS data for location-based gameplay, such as geocaching or location-based rewards.

4. Performance Considerations:

- **Touch Input Latency:** Minimize touch input latency by optimizing frame rates and input handling, ensuring that on-screen actions respond quickly to player touches.

- **Battery Optimization:** Implement power-efficient code and reduce background processes to extend battery life during gameplay.

5. Testing and User Feedback:

- **Device Testing:** Test your game on various mobile devices to ensure that touch controls are responsive and that the UI scales correctly.

- **User Testing:** Conduct usability testing with players to gather feedback on touch controls and mobile-specific features, making iterative improvements.

Code Example (Unity - Touch Input Handling):

Here's a simplified Unity C# script that demonstrates basic touch input handling for mobile controls:

```
using UnityEngine;

public class MobileTouchControls : MonoBehaviour
{
    private void Update()
    {
        // Check for touch input
        if (Input.touchCount > 0)
        {
            Touch touch = Input.GetTouch(0); // Get the first touch (assuming single-touch controls)

            // Check touch phases (began, moved, ended)
```

```
        if (touch.phase == TouchPhase.Began)
        {
            // Handle touch start
        }
        else if (touch.phase == TouchPhase.Moved)
        {
            // Handle touch movement
        }
        else if (touch.phase == TouchPhase.Ended)
        {
            // Handle touch end
        }
    }
  }
}
```

Conclusion:

Designing touch-friendly interfaces and incorporating mobile-specific features is crucial for creating successful mobile games with CryEngine. By following best practices for touch controls, UI design, and performance optimization, you can provide an enjoyable gaming experience for players on a wide range of mobile devices. Additionally, continually testing and iterating based on user feedback will help refine your game's mobile experience further.

Section 11.4: Deploying and Marketing Mobile Games

Deploying and marketing mobile games is a crucial aspect of the game development process. Once you have created your game using CryEngine, you need a strategy to publish it on various app stores, reach your target audience, and maximize its visibility. In this section, we'll explore the deployment and marketing strategies specific to mobile games.

1. Choosing App Stores:

- **Selecting Platforms:** Determine which mobile platforms (iOS, Android) your game will support. Each platform has its app store (Apple App Store, Google Play Store), so decide where to publish your game.

- **App Store Guidelines:** Familiarize yourself with the guidelines and policies of the chosen app stores to ensure your game complies with their requirements.

2. Pre-Launch Marketing:

- **Teaser Campaigns:** Start marketing your game well before its release. Teaser trailers, social media posts, and a dedicated website can build anticipation among potential players.

- **App Store Optimization (ASO):** Optimize your app store listings with relevant keywords, attractive screenshots, and engaging descriptions to improve discoverability.

3. Monetization Strategies:

- **In-App Purchases:** Consider implementing in-app purchases (IAPs) for virtual items, cosmetics, or premium features within your game.

- **Ads:** Incorporate mobile ad networks to display ads in your game. Options include interstitial, rewarded, and banner ads.

4. User Acquisition:

- **Paid User Acquisition:** Invest in paid advertising campaigns on platforms like Facebook, Google Ads, or mobile ad networks to acquire new users.

- **App Review Sites:** Submit your game to app review websites and influencers for coverage, reviews, and recommendations.

5. Community Engagement:

- **Social Media:** Maintain an active presence on social media platforms to engage with your community, share updates, and gather feedback.

- **Player Support:** Provide efficient customer support to address player inquiries, issues, and suggestions promptly.

6. Post-Launch Updates:

- **Regular Updates:** Plan and release regular updates to keep players engaged and address any bugs or issues.

- **Player Feedback:** Listen to player feedback and use it to enhance your game's features and content.

7. Analytics and Data:

- **Analytics Tools:** Utilize analytics tools to track user behavior, retention rates, and revenue sources. Adjust your marketing and development strategies based on data insights.

8. App Store Promotions:

- **Featuring Opportunities:** Strive to get your game featured by the app stores. Being featured can significantly boost downloads and visibility.

Code Example (Unity - Implementing Ads):

To implement ads in your mobile game, you can use a mobile ad network SDK. Here's a simplified example of how to integrate Unity's AdMob SDK for displaying banner ads:

```csharp
using UnityEngine;
using GoogleMobileAds.Api;

public class AdManager : MonoBehaviour
{
    private BannerView bannerAd;

    private void Start()
    {
        // Initialize the Mobile Ads SDK
        MobileAds.Initialize(initStatus => { });

        // Create a banner ad
        bannerAd = new BannerView("your-ad-unit-id", AdSize.Banner, AdPositio
n.Bottom);

        // Request an ad
        AdRequest request = new AdRequest.Builder().Build();
        bannerAd.LoadAd(request);
    }

    // Display the banner ad when needed
    public void ShowBannerAd()
    {
        bannerAd.Show();
    }

    // Hide the banner ad when not needed
    public void HideBannerAd()
    {
        bannerAd.Hide();
    }
}
```

Conclusion:

Deploying and marketing mobile games requires careful planning and execution. It's essential to understand the app store landscape, optimize your game's presence, engage with your audience, and use data-driven insights to refine your strategies. By following these guidelines and adapting them to your game's unique qualities, you can increase your mobile game's chances of success in a highly competitive market.

Section 11.5: Cross-Device Play and Integration

Cross-device play and integration have become increasingly important in the world of gaming. Enabling players to enjoy your game on various platforms, including mobile, PC, and consoles, can greatly enhance the user experience and expand your game's reach. In this section, we'll explore the concept of cross-device play, the technologies involved, and how to implement it effectively.

1. Understanding Cross-Device Play:

Cross-device play, also known as cross-platform play, allows gamers on different devices and platforms to play together in the same game environment. It promotes inclusivity and widens your game's player base.

2. Supported Platforms:

- **Identify Supported Platforms:** Determine which platforms you want to support for cross-device play. Common choices include PC, console (Xbox, PlayStation), and mobile (iOS, Android).

3. Technologies for Cross-Device Play:

- **APIs and SDKs:** Utilize cross-platform development tools and APIs to facilitate communication and data synchronization between different devices.

- **Cloud Services:** Cloud-based gaming services can enable seamless cross-device play by streaming game content to various devices.

4. User Accounts and Progress Sync:

- **Player Accounts:** Implement a player account system that allows users to create profiles and link them across different devices.

- **Progress Sync:** Sync player progress, achievements, and in-game purchases across platforms to maintain a consistent gaming experience.

5. Input and Controls:

- **Input Mapping:** Adapt input controls for each platform to ensure a fair and enjoyable experience. Touch controls for mobile, keyboard and mouse for PC, and gamepad support for consoles, for example.

6. Matchmaking and Player Pools:

- **Balanced Matchmaking:** Implement intelligent matchmaking systems that consider factors like player skill, platform, and input method to create fair matches.

- **Player Pools:** Merge player pools from different platforms to ensure a healthy player base and reduce waiting times for matches.

7. Game Updates and Cross-Platform Compatibility:

- **Timely Updates:** Ensure that game updates and patches are released simultaneously across all supported platforms to maintain synchronization.

- **Compatibility:** Pay attention to potential compatibility issues when new devices or platforms are introduced. Regularly test and adapt your game to maintain compatibility.

8. Player Communication:

- **Cross-Platform Chat:** Implement cross-platform chat systems or integrate with third-party chat services to enable communication between players on different devices.

9. Examples of Cross-Device Play:

- **Fortnite:** Epic Games' Fortnite is a prime example of successful cross-device play, allowing players on PC, consoles, and mobile devices to compete together.

- **Minecraft:** Minecraft offers cross-play between various platforms, fostering a collaborative and creative community.

10. Code Example (Unity - Cross-Device Input Handling):

To handle input from different devices in a Unity game, you can create a script to detect the current platform and adjust input accordingly:

```
using UnityEngine;

public class InputManager : MonoBehaviour
{
    private bool isMobile = false;

    private void Start()
    {
        // Detect the current platform
        isMobile = Application.isMobilePlatform;

        if (isMobile)
        {
            // Enable mobile-specific input settings
            // For example, enable touch controls
        }
        else
        {
            // Enable PC/console-specific input settings
            // For example, enable keyboard and mouse or gamepad controls
        }
    }
}
```

Conclusion:

Cross-device play and integration can significantly enhance the appeal of your game by allowing players from different platforms to connect and play together. By understanding the technologies involved, ensuring account and progress synchronization, adapting input controls, and addressing other considerations, you can create a seamless cross-device gaming experience that attracts a wider audience and keeps players engaged.

Chapter 12: Virtual Reality (VR) and Augmented Reality (AR)

Section 12.1: Developing High-End VR Games with CryEngine

Virtual Reality (VR) and Augmented Reality (AR) have revolutionized the way we experience and interact with digital content. In this section, we will delve into the exciting world of VR game development using CryEngine. We will explore the fundamentals of VR development, discuss best practices, and provide insights into creating high-end VR games that captivate and immerse players.

1. Understanding VR and CryEngine:

- **VR Basics:** Virtual Reality immerses players in a digital environment, providing a sense of presence and interaction. CryEngine's advanced rendering capabilities make it an excellent choice for VR development.

2. Setting Up CryEngine for VR:

- **Hardware Requirements:** Ensure that your development setup meets the hardware requirements for VR development, including compatible VR headsets and controllers.

- **CryEngine VR SDK:** Install the CryEngine VR SDK to access the necessary tools and assets for VR game development.

3. VR Design Considerations:

- **Comfort and Immersion:** Prioritize player comfort and immersion. Minimize motion sickness through careful design and optimization.

- **User Interface:** Create VR-friendly user interfaces that are easy to navigate in a 3D space. Consider motion-controlled menus and HUD elements.

4. VR Input and Interaction:

- **Motion Controllers:** Leverage motion controllers for realistic hand presence and interaction with in-game objects.

- **Physics and Interactivity:** Implement physics-based interactions that allow players to grab, manipulate, and interact with objects naturally.

5. VR Movement and Locomotion:

- **Locomotion Methods:** Explore different locomotion methods, such as teleportation, smooth locomotion, and room-scale movement, to accommodate player preferences.

- **Comfort Options:** Provide comfort settings to reduce motion sickness, such as snap-turning and adjustable movement speeds.

6. Optimizing for Performance:

- **Frame Rate:** Maintain a stable and high frame rate (usually 90Hz or above) to ensure a comfortable VR experience.

- **Rendering Optimization:** Optimize rendering settings and use techniques like level of detail (LOD) to maximize performance without compromising visual quality.

7. VR Audio Design:

- **3D Audio:** Utilize spatial audio to enhance immersion. Sound should come from the direction of its source, creating a realistic auditory environment.

- **Binaural Audio:** Implement binaural audio techniques to accurately simulate how sound is heard by human ears in 3D space.

8. Testing and QA:

- **VR Testing:** Extensive testing is crucial for VR experiences. Test on various VR platforms and gather feedback to fine-tune the experience.

9. Code Example (CryEngine - VR Input Handling):

To handle VR input in CryEngine, you can use CryAction's VR functions. Here's a simple example of detecting and responding to VR controller input:

```
function OnVRControllerButtonPress(controllerId, buttonId)
    if buttonId == VRButton.A then
        -- Handle the 'A' button press
    elseif buttonId == VRButton.B then
        -- Handle the 'B' button press
    end
end

CryAction.BindVRControllerButtonPress(OnVRControllerButtonPress)
```

Conclusion:

Developing high-end VR games with CryEngine opens up exciting possibilities for immersive experiences. By understanding the fundamentals of VR design, setting up CryEngine for VR, and considering input, interaction, and optimization, you can create VR games that captivate players and take them on incredible virtual adventures. VR development is a dynamic field, and staying up-to-date with the latest hardware and software advancements is essential to creating cutting-edge VR experiences.

Section 12.2: AR Game Development: Expanding Realities

Augmented Reality (AR) is a technology that overlays digital content onto the real world, blending the physical and virtual realms. In this section, we will explore AR game development using CryEngine, allowing you to create immersive and interactive experiences that enhance the real world with digital elements. We will cover the key aspects of AR game development, from understanding AR technology to practical implementation.

1. Understanding Augmented Reality:

- **AR Basics:** AR involves adding virtual objects or information to the user's real-world environment. It is often experienced through mobile devices, smart glasses, or AR headsets.

- **CryEngine and AR:** CryEngine's versatility and rendering capabilities make it a powerful tool for AR development.

2. Setting Up for AR Development:

- **AR Hardware:** Determine the target AR hardware for your project. Consider whether you're developing for mobile devices, smart glasses, or other AR platforms.

- **AR SDKs:** Explore AR software development kits (SDKs) compatible with CryEngine, such as ARCore (for Android) or ARKit (for iOS).

3. AR Design Considerations:

- **Real-World Integration:** Design AR experiences that seamlessly integrate with the user's environment, enhancing rather than disrupting it.

- **User Experience:** Prioritize user experience by ensuring that AR content is intuitive and responsive to real-world interactions.

4. AR Tracking and Recognition:

- **Object Tracking:** Implement object tracking to recognize real-world objects or images, allowing AR content to interact with them.

- **Marker-Based AR:** Utilize marker-based AR, where predefined markers trigger virtual content to appear when detected by the camera.

5. Interactivity and Input:

- **Gestures and Touch:** Integrate gestures and touch interactions to control and interact with AR objects.

- **Voice Commands:** Consider voice commands as a natural way for users to interact with AR content.

6. AR Content Creation:

- **3D Models:** Create 3D models and assets that seamlessly blend with the real world. Pay attention to lighting and shading for realistic integration.

- **Animations:** Animate AR objects to respond to user interactions or environmental changes.

7. Optimizing for AR Performance:

- **Frame Rate:** Maintain a smooth frame rate to prevent lag or stuttering in AR experiences.

- **Power Efficiency:** Optimize AR apps for power efficiency, especially on mobile devices, to extend battery life.

8. Testing and Calibration:

- **Device Calibration:** Calibrate AR apps to ensure accurate tracking and alignment with the real world.

- **Field Testing:** Conduct field tests in various real-world environments to assess AR performance and usability.

9. Code Example (CryEngine - AR Object Placement):

Here's a simplified example of how you can place an AR object in CryEngine based on real-world marker detection using ARCore (Android):

```
function OnMarkerDetected(markerId)
    -- Load and position the AR object relative to the detected marker.
    local arObject = LoadARObject("ar_object.cgf")
    local markerTransform = GetMarkerTransform(markerId)
    arObject:SetWorldTM(markerTransform)
end

ARCore.RegisterMarkerDetectionCallback(OnMarkerDetected)
```

Conclusion:

AR game development offers unique opportunities to blend the real and virtual worlds, creating captivating and interactive experiences. With CryEngine's capabilities and AR SDKs, you can develop AR games that engage users in innovative ways. Understanding AR fundamentals, setting up for AR development, and considering design, tracking, and interactivity are essential for successful AR game projects. As AR technology continues to evolve, staying updated with the latest advancements will enable you to push the boundaries of augmented reality gaming.

Section 12.3: Implementing Interactive VR/AR Environments

In this section, we'll delve into the development of interactive Virtual Reality (VR) and Augmented Reality (AR) environments using CryEngine. Interactive environments are a key component of immersive VR and AR experiences, as they allow users to engage with the virtual world in meaningful ways. Whether you're designing a VR game or an AR application, creating interactive environments enhances user engagement and immersion.

1. Understanding Interactive VR/AR Environments:

- **Interactivity Definition:** Interactive VR/AR environments refer to digital spaces where users can manipulate objects, trigger events, or interact with the virtual world through various input methods.

- **Importance of Interactivity:** Interactivity is a fundamental aspect of VR/AR experiences, as it fosters user engagement and contributes to a sense of presence.

2. Designing Interactive Elements:

- **User-Centric Design:** Prioritize user-centered design by considering how users will interact with the environment. Identify user goals and design interactive elements that align with these goals.

- **Spatial Considerations:** In VR, spatial design is crucial. Ensure that interactive elements are appropriately positioned in 3D space and that users can reach them comfortably.

3. Input Mechanisms:

- **VR/AR Input Devices:** Depending on the platform, users may interact with VR/AR environments using controllers, hand gestures, voice commands, or touch inputs. Implement the appropriate input mechanisms for your target platform.

- **Gesture Recognition:** Develop gesture recognition systems that allow users to perform actions like grabbing, pointing, or swiping to interact with objects.

4. Physics and Interaction Models:

- **Physics Simulation:** Integrate physics engines to create realistic interactions between objects in the environment. Objects should behave naturally when touched or manipulated.

- **Interaction Models:** Define interaction models that determine how objects respond to user input. For example, you may implement a "pick up and throw" interaction model for objects.

5. Scripting and Event Handling:

- **Event-Based Interactions:** Implement event-driven interactions. Events can be triggered by user actions, such as pressing a button or touching an object.

- **Scripting Languages:** Utilize scripting languages supported by CryEngine (e.g., Lua) to create interactive behavior. Write scripts that handle events and interactions.

6. User Feedback:

- **Visual Feedback:** Provide visual cues to indicate the results of user interactions. For example, change the color of an object when it's selected or highlight interactive elements.

- **Haptic Feedback:** If the VR/AR hardware supports it, consider haptic feedback to provide tactile sensations during interactions.

7. Code Example (CryEngine - VR Object Interaction):

Here's a simplified example of how you can implement object interaction in a VR environment using CryEngine and C++:

```cpp
void OnControllerButtonPress(EntityId controller, ButtonId button)
{
    if (button == ButtonId::Trigger)
    {
        // Determine the object the controller is pointing at.
        EntityId objectInSight = RaycastFromController(controller);

        if (objectInSight != INVALID_ENTITY_ID)
        {
            // Trigger an interaction event with the object.
            InteractiveObjectScript::OnInteract(objectInSight);
        }
    }
}
```

Conclusion:

Creating interactive VR/AR environments is a critical aspect of immersive experiences. Users expect to engage with the virtual world through natural interactions. By understanding the importance of interactivity, designing user-centric elements, implementing appropriate input mechanisms, incorporating physics and interaction models, scripting event handling, providing feedback, and following best practices, you can develop compelling VR/AR environments that captivate and engage users. The integration of interactive elements enhances the overall quality and appeal of VR/AR applications and games, making them more enjoyable and immersive.

Section 12.4: Overcoming Challenges in VR/AR Development

Developing Virtual Reality (VR) and Augmented Reality (AR) experiences presents unique challenges that require careful consideration and innovative solutions. In this section, we'll explore some of the common challenges faced by VR/AR developers and strategies to overcome them.

1. Hardware Limitations:

- **Challenge:** VR/AR experiences are highly dependent on the capabilities of the hardware. Variations in hardware specifications, such as processing power, display quality, and tracking accuracy, can impact the user experience.

- **Solution:** Developers should optimize their applications to perform well on a range of hardware configurations. Use adaptive graphics settings and consider scalability in design.

2. Motion Sickness:

- **Challenge:** Motion sickness is a significant concern in VR experiences. Rapid movements and mismatch between virtual and physical motion can lead to discomfort for users.

- **Solution:** Implement comfort features like teleportation, snap turning, and gradual acceleration to reduce motion sickness. Conduct user testing to refine these features.

3. User Interface (UI) Design:

- **Challenge:** Designing user interfaces that are intuitive and functional in VR/AR can be challenging. Traditional 2D UI elements may not translate well to immersive environments.

- **Solution:** Create spatial UIs that integrate seamlessly with the environment. Use gaze-based interactions and 3D menus to enhance usability.

4. Content Creation:

- **Challenge:** Creating 3D content for VR/AR can be time-consuming and resource-intensive. Developing high-quality assets and animations can pose challenges.

- **Solution:** Employ tools and software that streamline 3D asset creation and animation. Collaborate with artists experienced in VR/AR content creation.

5. User Comfort:

- **Challenge:** Ensuring user comfort is essential. VR/AR experiences should not induce discomfort, eye strain, or fatigue.

- **Solution:** Optimize frame rates and resolution to reduce eye strain. Implement comfort settings that allow users to customize their experience.

6. Testing and Feedback:

- **Challenge:** Comprehensive testing is critical, but it can be difficult to gather user feedback, especially during early development stages.

- **Solution:** Conduct regular playtesting with a diverse group of users. Collect feedback on comfort, usability, and overall experience to make iterative improvements.

7. Performance Optimization:

- **Challenge:** Maintaining consistent performance is crucial for VR/AR applications. Poor performance can break immersion.

- **Solution:** Profile and optimize code, use level of detail (LOD) techniques for 3D models, and employ occlusion culling to improve performance.

8. User Interaction:

- **Challenge:** Designing natural and intuitive interactions can be complex. Users expect realistic interactions with virtual objects.

- **Solution:** Implement hand tracking, haptic feedback, and physics-based interactions to make VR/AR experiences more immersive.

9. Accessibility:

- **Challenge:** Ensuring that VR/AR experiences are accessible to users with disabilities can be overlooked.

- **Solution:** Design with accessibility in mind. Provide options for users with different needs, such as text-to-speech support or alternative input methods.

10. Software and SDK Updates:

- **Challenge:** VR/AR hardware and software ecosystems are rapidly evolving. Keeping up with updates and changes can be challenging.

- **Solution:** Stay informed about updates to VR/AR platforms and SDKs. Allocate time for adaptation when major changes occur.

11. Deployment and Distribution:

- **Challenge:** Distributing VR/AR applications to users can be complex, especially across multiple platforms.

- **Solution:** Explore distribution channels, app stores, and cross-platform deployment tools to reach your target audience effectively.

Conclusion:

VR/AR development offers incredible opportunities for immersive experiences, but it comes with its unique set of challenges. Overcoming these challenges requires a combination of technical expertise, user-centered design, and adaptability to evolving technologies. By addressing hardware limitations, mitigating motion sickness, refining UI design, streamlining content creation, prioritizing user comfort, conducting thorough testing, optimizing performance, enhancing user interaction, ensuring accessibility, staying updated, and mastering distribution, developers can create compelling and successful VR/AR applications that captivate and engage users.

Section 12.5: Future Trends in VR/AR Gaming

As technology continues to advance, the landscape of Virtual Reality (VR) and Augmented Reality (AR) gaming is evolving rapidly. In this section, we'll explore some of the exciting trends and developments that are shaping the future of VR/AR gaming.

1. Improved Hardware:

- The ongoing development of more powerful and affordable VR/AR hardware is making immersive experiences accessible to a broader audience. Upcoming headsets are expected to feature higher resolutions, wider fields of view, and improved tracking accuracy, further enhancing the sense of presence.

2. Wireless and Standalone VR/AR:

- The trend towards wireless and standalone VR/AR devices is gaining momentum. These devices eliminate the need for cumbersome cables and external sensors, providing users with greater freedom of movement and ease of use.

3. Mixed Reality (MR):

- Mixed Reality combines elements of both AR and VR, allowing users to interact with virtual objects while still being aware of the physical world. MR headsets and experiences are becoming more prevalent, opening up new possibilities for gaming and productivity applications.

4. Social VR/AR:

- Social interaction is a key driver of VR/AR gaming's future. Developers are creating multiplayer and social experiences where players can meet, interact, and collaborate in virtual spaces. This trend is expected to grow as technology improves.

5. Natural User Interfaces:

- VR/AR is moving towards more intuitive and natural user interfaces. Hand tracking, gesture recognition, and voice commands are becoming standard features, making interactions with virtual environments more lifelike.

6. Haptic Feedback and Sensory Experiences:

- Developers are exploring haptic feedback technologies to provide users with tactile sensations in VR/AR. This enhances immersion by simulating touch, force, and even temperature changes.

7. Realistic Physics and Simulation:

- Advances in physics simulation allow for more realistic interactions with virtual objects and environments. This is particularly relevant in gaming genres such as physics-based puzzles and simulations.

8. AI and Machine Learning:

- AI-driven NPCs and dynamic content generation are becoming integral to VR/AR gaming. Machine learning techniques enhance realism and adaptability, creating more immersive and challenging experiences.

9. Health and Wellness Applications:

- VR/AR is increasingly being used in health and wellness applications, including physical therapy, fitness, and stress reduction. Gaming experiences that promote physical activity and well-being are on the rise.

10. Cross-Platform Play:

- Developers are focusing on enabling cross-platform play, allowing users on different VR/AR platforms to interact and play together seamlessly. This fosters larger player communities and extends the life of VR/AR games.

11. Content Diversity:

- VR/AR gaming is diversifying beyond traditional gaming genres. Educational, artistic, and experiential applications are emerging, appealing to a broader audience and expanding the potential use cases.

12. Cloud Gaming and Streaming:

- Cloud gaming services are exploring VR/AR support, allowing users to access high-quality VR/AR experiences without the need for powerful local hardware. This could democratize access to VR/AR content.

13. Ethical Considerations:

- As VR/AR experiences become more immersive, ethical considerations around content, privacy, and psychological effects are gaining attention. Developers and regulators are working to establish guidelines and standards.

Conclusion:

The future of VR/AR gaming holds tremendous promise, with ongoing advancements in hardware, user interfaces, social interactions, and content diversity. As these technologies become more accessible and immersive, VR/AR gaming is poised to reshape the way we play, learn, and interact with digital environments. Developers, content creators, and enthusiasts have an exciting journey ahead as they explore these trends and push the boundaries of what is possible in the world of virtual and augmented reality gaming.

Chapter 13: Procedural Generation for Dynamic Gameplay

Section 13.1: Advanced Techniques in Procedural Generation

Procedural generation is a powerful tool in game development that allows for the creation of dynamic and ever-changing game worlds and content. In this section, we will delve into advanced techniques in procedural generation, exploring how they can be used to enhance gameplay and create unique player experiences.

1. Perlin Noise and Fractal Landscapes:

- Perlin noise is a fundamental technique in procedural generation used to create natural-looking terrains, textures, and patterns. Combining multiple layers of Perlin noise can generate complex and realistic landscapes, which is especially useful in open-world games.

2. Cellular Automata:

- Cellular automata are mathematical models used to simulate the behavior of cellular structures. In game development, they can be employed to create natural phenomena like vegetation growth, spreading diseases, or even simulating crowds and traffic patterns.

3. L-Systems for Organic Structures:

- L-Systems, or Lindenmayer systems, are used to model the growth of organic structures such as trees, plants, or coral reefs. Game developers utilize L-Systems to procedurally generate detailed and visually appealing flora in game environments.

4. Dungeon Generation:

- Procedural dungeon generation is a classic application of procedural content generation. It involves creating randomized layouts for dungeons, caves, or mazes, ensuring that each playthrough offers a unique challenge for players.

5. Biome and Ecosystem Simulation:

- Procedural generation can simulate entire ecosystems with different biomes, weather patterns, and wildlife. This approach is used in survival and exploration games to create diverse and living game worlds.

6. Quest and Narrative Generation:

- Procedural generation techniques can extend to creating quests, missions, and narratives. Dynamic story generation ensures that players encounter unique challenges and experiences during their playthroughs.

7. Population and Civilization Simulation:

- In strategy and simulation games, procedural generation can simulate the growth and behavior of populations and civilizations. This allows for dynamic world-building and strategic depth.

8. Resource Distribution:

- Procedurally generated resource distribution is crucial for resource management games. It ensures that the availability and placement of resources evolve over time, influencing gameplay decisions.

9. Texture and Material Variation:

- Procedural generation can be used to create variations in textures and materials, making objects and surfaces appear weathered, aged, or customized. This adds visual richness to game environments.

10. Music and Soundscapes:

- Beyond visuals, procedural generation extends to audio. Dynamic music and soundscapes adapt to in-game events and player actions, enhancing immersion and emotional engagement.

11. Realistic Flora and Fauna:

- Procedural generation can simulate ecosystems with realistic behaviors for flora and fauna. This includes predator-prey relationships, migration patterns, and environmental adaptations.

12. Error Handling and Consistency:

- When implementing procedural generation, it's essential to handle errors and ensure consistency in the generated content. This involves managing edge cases and maintaining the balance of gameplay elements.

13. User-Created Content:

- Procedural generation can also empower players to create and share their content. Games with robust procedural content creation tools allow players to contribute to the game's world and share their creations with others.

14. Challenges in Procedural Generation:

- While powerful, procedural generation is not without its challenges. Developers must address issues like content quality, player frustration, and ensuring that procedurally generated content feels coherent and meaningful.

15. Playtesting and Iteration:

- Playtesting is crucial when using procedural generation. It helps identify issues, refine algorithms, and ensure that procedurally generated content aligns with the game's design and player expectations.

16. Ethical Considerations:

- Procedural generation can inadvertently produce offensive or harmful content. Developers must consider ethical implications and implement safeguards to prevent such content from reaching players.

In conclusion, advanced techniques in procedural generation offer game developers a wide array of tools to create dynamic and engaging gameplay experiences. Whether it's crafting vast open worlds, generating intricate narrative structures, or simulating complex ecosystems, procedural generation continues to push the boundaries of what is possible in game design, ensuring that each playthrough is a unique and memorable journey for players.

Section 13.2: Creating Infinite Game Worlds

Creating infinite game worlds using procedural generation is an exciting challenge that offers players vast, ever-expanding environments to explore. This section explores various techniques and considerations for generating infinite game worlds.

1. Random Seed Generation:**

- Infinite worlds often start with a random seed that serves as the initial state for procedural generation algorithms. By changing the seed, you can create entirely new worlds, ensuring that players never run out of fresh content.

2. Tiling and Chunking:**

- To efficiently manage infinite worlds, developers divide them into smaller tiles or chunks. Each tile represents a portion of the world, and only the tiles close to the player are actively generated and loaded. This approach reduces memory usage and speeds up generation.

3. Terrain Generation:**

- Terrain generation in infinite worlds can use Perlin noise or other algorithms to create realistic landscapes with mountains, valleys, rivers, and more. These algorithms ensure that the terrain seamlessly extends beyond the player's view.

4. Biome and Climate Simulation:**

- Infinite worlds often feature multiple biomes and climates. Procedural generation can simulate these environments, including temperature, precipitation, and vegetation, to create diverse and immersive landscapes.

5. Dynamic Population:**

- In infinite worlds, the population of creatures, NPCs, and resources can be procedurally controlled. Creatures migrate, resources replenish, and NPC settlements expand or contract based on dynamic algorithms.

6. Cave and Dungeon Generation:**

- Procedural generation extends to subterranean spaces, creating caves, dungeons, and underground structures. These areas can be seamlessly integrated into the infinite world, offering exploration and challenges.

7. Infinite Oceans and Water Bodies:**

- Infinite worlds can feature vast oceans, lakes, and rivers. Procedural generation ensures that water bodies extend infinitely, offering opportunities for naval exploration and aquatic gameplay.

8. Realistic Day-Night Cycles:**

- Implementing a realistic day-night cycle in infinite worlds requires procedural generation of the sky, sun, moon, and stars. This adds to the immersion and provides strategic gameplay elements.

9. Resource Distribution:**

- Resources like ores, minerals, and vegetation need to be distributed consistently across the infinite world. Procedural generation algorithms control the placement, abundance, and regeneration of these resources.

10. Player Interaction and Modification:**

- Players often have the ability to modify the world through building, mining, or other actions. Procedural generation algorithms must adapt to player changes and ensure the world remains coherent.

11. Limiting and Controlling World Size:**

- Despite being "infinite," developers may want to limit the size of the playable world to keep gameplay engaging and manageable. This requires implementing mechanisms to control world size and prevent it from becoming unmanageable.

12. Performance Optimization:**

- Infinite worlds present performance challenges. Developers must optimize algorithms, use level-of-detail techniques, and implement efficient data structures to ensure smooth gameplay and manageable memory usage.

13. Seamless Transitions:**

- When players move from one chunk to another, seamless transitions are essential. Procedural generation algorithms should ensure that there are no jarring changes in terrain, climate, or resources at chunk boundaries.

14. Multiplayer Considerations:**

```
- In multiplayer games with infinite worlds, synchronization and network opti
mization become critical. Players should see the same world state and interac
t with it consistently.
```

15. Persistence and Saving:**

```
- Infinite worlds need robust persistence and saving mechanisms. This ensures
that player progress and world changes are stored and loaded correctly across
sessions.
```

16. User-Generated Content:**

```
- Some games allow players to contribute to the generation of infinite worlds
, creating a collaborative and ever-evolving experience. This involves implem
enting tools and systems for user-generated content.
```

Creating infinite game worlds through procedural generation is a complex but rewarding endeavor. When executed well, it provides players with endless exploration opportunities, making each playthrough a unique and exciting journey. Developers must carefully balance realism, performance, and gameplay to deliver a seamless and immersive experience in these vast and limitless digital landscapes.

Section 13.3: Procedural Puzzles and Challenges

Incorporating procedural puzzles and challenges into your game can add depth and variety to gameplay. This section explores the concept of procedural puzzle generation, discusses different types of puzzles, and provides insights into implementing them effectively.

1. Procedural Puzzle Generation:**

- Procedural puzzles are generated dynamically, ensuring that players encounter new challenges in each playthrough. This approach keeps gameplay fresh and prevents players from memorizing solutions.

2. Types of Procedural Puzzles:**

- There are various types of procedural puzzles, including logic puzzles, riddles, platforming challenges, mazes, and environmental puzzles. Each type requires different generation techniques.

3. Logic Puzzles:**

- Logic puzzles involve deducing a solution using reasoning and deduction. Procedural generation can create puzzles with randomized elements, such as Sudoku grids or circuitry configurations.

163

4. Riddles and Clues:**

- Riddles and clue-based puzzles provide cryptic hints that players must decipher to progress. Procedural generation can create unique riddles and clues, ensuring that players face novel challenges.

5. Platforming Challenges:**

- Procedurally generated platforming challenges involve creating sequences of platforms, obstacles, and traps. Algorithms can adjust difficulty based on player skill or progression.

6. Mazes and Labyrinths:**

- Mazes and labyrinths can be procedurally generated with varying complexity. They can serve as exploration challenges or be integrated into the game's narrative.

7. Environmental Puzzles:**

- Environmental puzzles require players to interact with the game world creatively. Procedural generation can create dynamic environments with interactive elements, such as moving platforms or physics-based puzzles.

8. Randomized Solutions:**

- In procedural puzzles, solutions should not follow fixed patterns. Instead, they should be generated randomly within predefined constraints, ensuring that players cannot predict outcomes.

9. Balancing Difficulty:**

- Procedural puzzle generation algorithms must include difficulty parameters. These parameters can be adjusted to match the player's skill level or the game's progression.

10. Integration with Narrative:**

- Procedural puzzles can be seamlessly integrated into the game's narrative, enhancing the storytelling experience. For example, solving a puzzle might reveal a piece of the game's lore or advance the plot.

11. Feedback and Iteration:**

- Testing and player feedback are crucial for refining procedurally generated puzzles. Developers should iterate on their generation algorithms based on player experiences.

12. Dynamic Puzzle Generation:**

- Some games employ dynamic puzzle generation that adapts to player decisions and actions. This creates a personalized challenge and prevents players from relying on walkthroughs.

13. User-Created Puzzles:**

- Allowing players to create and share their procedural puzzles can extend th
e game's lifespan. User-generated content adds a community aspect to puzzle-s
olving.

14. Performance Considerations:**

- Procedurally generating complex puzzles in real-time may impact game perfor
mance. Developers must optimize algorithms to ensure smooth gameplay.

15. Accessibility and Inclusivity:**

- Consider accessibility options for puzzles to accommodate players with diff
erent abilities. Some players may prefer alternative puzzle-solving methods o
r require additional hints.

16. Combining Procedural Puzzles:**

- Complex gameplay experiences can emerge by combining different types of pro
cedural puzzles within a game. This can create rich, multifaceted challenges.

Procedural puzzle generation is a powerful tool for enhancing gameplay variety and
replayability. When implemented thoughtfully, it can provide players with enjoyable and
intellectually stimulating experiences. Balancing difficulty, integrating puzzles with the
narrative, and considering accessibility are essential aspects of creating procedurally
generated puzzles that resonate with players and contribute to the overall success of a
game.

Section 13.4: AI-Driven Content Creation

Artificial Intelligence (AI) has revolutionized the field of content creation in the gaming
industry. This section delves into how AI can be leveraged to generate game content
dynamically, from environments and characters to quests and storylines.

1. Procedural Content vs. AI-Driven Content:**

- Procedural content generation primarily relies on algorithms and predefined rules
  to create content, whereas AI-driven content creation utilizes machine learning
  models and data-driven approaches.

2. Generating Environments:**

- AI can be employed to generate vast and realistic game environments. Machine
  learning models can analyze real-world data, such as satellite images, to create
  terrain, vegetation, and structures.

3. Creating NPCs and Characters:**

- AI-driven character generation involves creating non-player characters (NPCs) with unique personalities, behaviors, and appearances. Generative models can simulate human-like traits and voices.

4. Dynamic Quest Generation:**

- AI can generate quests and missions based on player choices and actions. This dynamic quest system adapts to player progression and creates personalized experiences.

5. Storyline and Dialog Generation:**

- Natural language processing (NLP) models enable the generation of interactive dialogues, branching narratives, and compelling storylines. AI can respond to player choices in real-time.

6. Balancing and Fair Play:**

- AI-driven content generation considers game balance and fairness. It adjusts the difficulty of generated challenges based on player skill, ensuring an engaging experience for all players.

7. Content Validation:**

- AI can validate generated content to ensure it aligns with the game's design and quality standards. This includes checking for bugs, glitches, and inconsistencies.

8. Data and Training:**

- AI-driven content generation relies on extensive data and training. Game developers need access to relevant datasets and must fine-tune AI models to suit their specific game.

9. AI Content Tools:**

- Several AI content creation tools and frameworks, such as GANs (Generative Adversarial Networks) and reinforcement learning, are available for game developers to use or build upon.

10. Procedural vs. AI-Driven Hybrids:**

- Some games combine procedural generation with AI-driven content creation. This hybrid approach allows for greater creativity and control over the generated content.

11. Player-Driven Content:**

- AI can enable player-driven content creation within games. Players can train AI models to generate custom content or modify existing game assets.

12. Ethical Considerations:**

- Developers must consider ethical implications when using AI for content creation. This includes addressing biases in AI models and ensuring responsible use of AI-generated content.

13. Performance Optimization:**

- AI-driven content generation may require substantial computational resources. Developers should optimize algorithms to maintain smooth gameplay.

14. Player Engagement:**

- AI-generated content should aim to enhance player engagement and immersion. It should feel seamlessly integrated into the game world.

15. Future Trends:**

- The field of AI-driven content creation is rapidly evolving. Developers should stay updated on emerging AI technologies and their potential applications in game development.

AI-driven content creation represents a paradigm shift in game development, offering the potential for endless content possibilities and dynamic player experiences. Leveraging AI for content generation requires a deep understanding of machine learning techniques, access to relevant data, and a commitment to ethical considerations. As AI continues to advance, it will play an increasingly pivotal role in shaping the future of game content creation.

Section 13.5: Balancing Randomization with Design

Balancing the use of randomization in game design is a critical aspect of creating engaging and enjoyable gameplay experiences. Random elements can add variety, challenge, and replayability to games, but excessive or poorly implemented randomness can frustrate players. This section explores strategies for effectively balancing randomization with intentional design in game development.

1. Randomization in Games:**

- Randomization is the introduction of unpredictable elements into a game. This can include random enemy spawns, loot drops, level layouts, and more.

2. Benefits of Randomization:**

- Randomization can make each playthrough of a game unique, keeping players engaged and encouraging replayability.

3. Challenges of Randomization:**

- Excessive randomness can lead to frustration if players feel that their success or failure is purely luck-based. Balancing is essential.

4. Intentional Design:**

- Game designers should carefully consider where and how to incorporate random elements into gameplay to serve specific design goals.

5. Balancing Difficulty:**

- Randomization can be used to adjust the difficulty of a game dynamically. For example, increasing enemy aggression when a player is performing well.

6. Reward Systems:**

- Randomized rewards, such as loot drops, can create excitement and anticipation. However, designers should ensure that rewards are balanced and feel earned.

7. Player Agency:**

- Balancing randomization with player agency is crucial. Players should feel that their decisions and skill contribute to their success.

8. Risk and Reward:**

- Randomized outcomes can create risk and reward scenarios. Players may take calculated risks for potentially valuable rewards.

9. Progression Systems:**

- Randomization can be used in progression systems, such as skill trees or item crafting, to provide variety and customization options.

10. Testing and Iteration:**

- Game designers should playtest randomized elements extensively to find the right balance. Iteration based on player feedback is essential.

11. Player Skill vs. Randomness:**

- Balancing the impact of player skill and randomness is critical. Skillful p lay should generally lead to success, but random elements can introduce surpr ises.

12. Transparency:**

- Games should communicate the presence of random elements to players so they can make informed decisions.

13. Adaptive AI and Difficulty Scaling:**

- AI-driven by adaptive algorithms can adjust difficulty based on player perf ormance, achieving a balance between challenge and fairness.

14. Fairness and Frustration:**

- Designers must avoid situations where excessive randomness causes unfair or frustrating experiences.

15. Game Genres and Randomization:**

- The appropriate use of randomization varies by game genre. For example, roguelike games heavily rely on randomization for their core gameplay loop.

16. Community Feedback:**

- Engaging with the gaming community and gathering feedback is crucial for identifying areas where randomization needs adjustment.

17. Ethical Considerations:**

- When implementing microtransactions or loot boxes with random rewards, developers should adhere to ethical guidelines and regulations.

18. Dynamic Storytelling:**

- Random elements can impact the narrative in games. Balancing story-driven elements with randomness requires careful planning.

19. The Art of Surprise:**

- Well-balanced randomness can create surprising and memorable moments that players cherish.

20. Future Trends:**

- As technology advances, game designers will have more tools and techniques at their disposal for balancing randomization and design effectively.

Balancing randomization with design is a delicate art in game development. When done well, it can elevate a game's enjoyment and replayability. However, designers must tread carefully to ensure that random elements enhance the player's experience rather than hinder it. As the gaming industry continues to evolve, finding the right balance between skill, strategy, and randomness will remain a fundamental challenge for game developers.

Chapter 14: Data-Driven Game Design

Section 14.1: Leveraging Analytics for Game Development

In today's gaming industry, data-driven game design has become an integral part of creating successful and engaging games. Leveraging analytics and player data allows game developers to make informed decisions, improve player experiences, and optimize game performance. This section explores the role of analytics in game development and how it can be used to enhance various aspects of game design.

1. The Importance of Data:**

- Analytics provides valuable insights into player behavior, preferences, and interactions within a game.

2. Player-Centric Approach:**

- Data-driven game design prioritizes understanding player needs and expectations.

3. Key Metrics:**

- Game developers track metrics such as player retention, engagement, monetization, and more to assess game performance.

4. A/B Testing:**

- A/B testing involves comparing two versions of a game feature to determine which one performs better based on player data.

5. Player Segmentation:**

- Analyzing player data allows developers to segment players into groups with similar behavior and tailor game experiences accordingly.

6. Balancing Gameplay:**

- Analytics helps identify imbalances in gameplay, allowing developers to adjust difficulty and progression.

7. Content Creation:**

- Data-driven insights guide content creation, helping developers prioritize features and updates that resonate with players.

8. Monetization Strategies:**

- Understanding player spending patterns informs the design of in-game purchases and monetization strategies.

9. Predictive Analytics:**

- Predictive analytics can forecast player behavior and inform long-term game development strategies.

10. Real-Time Analytics:**

- Some games use real-time analytics to react to player actions and adjust gameplay dynamically.

11. Player Feedback Integration:**

- Combining player feedback with analytics data provides a holistic view of player sentiment and issues.

12. Ethical Considerations:**

- Developers must use player data responsibly, respecting privacy and avoiding exploitative practices.

13. Tools and Platforms:**

- Various analytics tools and platforms are available for game developers to collect and analyze data.

14. Iterative Development:**

- Data-driven development is an iterative process, with continuous data collection and refinement.

15. Balancing Art and Data:**

- Game developers must strike a balance between creative design and data-driven decision-making.

16. Post-Launch Optimization:**

- Analytics remain crucial after a game's release for ongoing updates and improvements.

17. Player Behavior Patterns:**

- Identifying patterns in player behavior helps tailor game experiences to different player segments.

18. Cohort Analysis:**

- Cohort analysis allows developers to track the performance of groups of players over time.

19. Learning from Data:**

- Game development teams should foster a culture of learning and adaptability based on analytics insights.

20. Future Trends:**

- As technology advances, analytics will play an even larger role in shaping the future of game design and development.

In conclusion, analytics is a powerful tool that empowers game developers to create better, more engaging, and financially successful games. It allows developers to understand player behavior, adapt gameplay, and make data-informed decisions throughout the game development lifecycle. As the gaming industry continues to evolve, the integration of analytics into game design and development processes will remain essential for delivering outstanding gaming experiences.

Section 14.2: Player Behavior Analysis and Engagement Strategies

Understanding player behavior is a crucial aspect of data-driven game design. By analyzing how players interact with your game, you can gain insights that help improve player engagement, retention, and overall satisfaction. In this section, we'll delve into the process of player behavior analysis and explore strategies for enhancing player engagement.

1. Data Collection:

- To analyze player behavior, you need to collect relevant data. This includes in-game actions, playtime, progression, and interactions.

2. Player Segmentation:

- Segment your player base into groups based on behavior, demographics, or other criteria. This allows you to tailor strategies to different player segments.

3. Metrics and KPIs:

- Define key performance indicators (KPIs) and metrics that align with your game's goals. Common metrics include daily active users (DAU), monthly active users (MAU), retention rate, and churn rate.

4. Funnel Analysis:

- Funnel analysis tracks how players progress through specific sequences of actions in your game. It can reveal bottlenecks or areas where players drop off.

5. Heatmaps:

- Heatmaps visually represent player activity within levels or screens. They can highlight popular areas or interactions and areas that players avoid.

6. Cohort Analysis:

- Cohort analysis groups players who started at the same time or under similar conditions. It helps track player retention and engagement over time.

7. A/B Testing:

- A/B testing allows you to experiment with different game features or changes to see which ones have a positive impact on player behavior.

8. Player Feedback:

- Consider feedback from players, including surveys, reviews, and direct communication. Player feedback can provide qualitative insights into their preferences and pain points.

9. Player Journeys:

- Analyze the complete player journey from onboarding to long-term engagement. Identify critical points where players may become disengaged.

10. Predictive Modeling:

- Use predictive modeling to forecast future player behavior, such as predicting churn or spending patterns. This can inform targeted interventions.

11. Social Interaction Analysis:

- Examine how players interact with each other within the game. Encouraging social interactions can boost engagement.

12. Personalization:

- Tailor in-game experiences based on individual player behavior and preferences. Personalization can increase player satisfaction.

13. Monetization Insights:

- Analyze spending patterns and purchase behavior to optimize in-game monetization strategies.

14. Event Tracking:

- Implement event tracking to record specific player actions and interactions. This can provide granular insights into behavior.

15. Retention Strategies:

- Develop strategies to retain players over the long term. This may involve introducing regular content updates, events, or rewards.

16. Behavioral Economics:

- Leverage principles of behavioral economics to design in-game incentives and rewards that encourage desired player behavior.

17. Balancing Act:

- Balancing the need for player engagement with ethical considerations is crucial. Avoid manipulative practices that exploit players.

18. Feedback Loops:

- Implement feedback loops based on player behavior analysis. Iterate on your game's design and features to improve the player experience.

19. Continuous Improvement:

- Player behavior analysis should be an ongoing process. Regularly review and update your strategies based on new data and player feedback.

20. Ethical Considerations:

- Always prioritize the ethical use of player data. Transparency and player consent are essential in data collection and analysis.

In summary, player behavior analysis is a dynamic and iterative process that enables game developers to create more engaging and player-centric experiences. By collecting and analyzing data, segmenting players, and implementing targeted strategies, you can enhance player engagement, improve retention, and create a more enjoyable gaming environment. Remember to strike a balance between optimizing player behavior and ensuring ethical and fair gameplay practices.

Section 14.3: Implementing Data-Driven Decisions in Game Design

In the era of data-driven game development, making informed decisions based on player data is essential for creating successful and engaging games. In this section, we will explore how to implement data-driven decisions in various aspects of game design.

1. Player Data Collection:

- To begin making data-driven decisions, you need to collect relevant player data. This includes gameplay metrics, player behavior, and feedback.

2. Define Clear Objectives:

- Determine specific objectives or goals for your game. Are you aiming to increase player retention, monetization, or engagement? Define what success means for your game.

3. Key Performance Indicators (KPIs):

- Identify and monitor key performance indicators that align with your objectives. KPIs can include metrics like daily active users (DAU), average session length, conversion rates, and more.

4. Hypothesis Generation:

- Formulate hypotheses or assumptions based on your KPIs and objectives. For example, if your goal is to increase retention, you might hypothesize that improving the onboarding experience will achieve this.

5. A/B Testing:

- Implement A/B testing to compare different versions or features of your game. This controlled experimentation helps validate or refute hypotheses by analyzing how changes impact player behavior.

6. User Feedback Integration:

- Incorporate player feedback, both qualitative and quantitative, into your decision-making process. Feedback can reveal pain points and insights that data alone may not capture.

7. Iterative Design:

- Embrace an iterative design process that allows you to make incremental changes based on data and feedback. Continuously refine and optimize your game.

8. Content Updates:

- Regularly release content updates, patches, or new features based on player data and preferences. This keeps the game fresh and players engaged.

9. Player Segmentation:

- Segment your player base into distinct groups with similar characteristics or behaviors. This allows for tailored design decisions and marketing strategies.

10. Monetization Strategies:

- Analyze player spending patterns and adjust monetization strategies accordingly. Data can help determine the most effective pricing models and in-game purchases.

11. Balancing and Difficulty:

- Use data to fine-tune the game's balance and difficulty levels. Analyze player progression and adjust challenges to maintain engagement without frustrating players.

12. Player Retention:

- Implement strategies to improve player retention, such as rewards, events, or social features, based on data indicating where players tend to drop off.

13. Live Ops and Events:

- Create live operations and in-game events informed by player behavior and p
references. These events can boost player engagement and monetization.

14. Ethical Considerations:

- While data-driven decisions are valuable, maintain ethical practices in dat
a collection and use. Ensure transparency and respect for player privacy.

15. Player-Centric Approach:

- Always prioritize the player experience. Use data to enhance player satisfa
ction and enjoyment, rather than solely focusing on metrics.

16. Regular Monitoring:

- Continuously monitor player data to detect trends and anomalies. Stay agile
and be ready to adapt your design decisions accordingly.

17. Data-Driven Culture:

- Foster a data-driven culture within your development team. Encourage data a
nalysis and decision-making at all levels of game development.

18. Player Lifetime Value (LTV):

- Calculate and optimize player lifetime value to understand the long-term im
pact of your decisions on player engagement and revenue.

19. Documentation:

- Keep records of your data-driven decisions, including the rationale behind
each change. This documentation helps maintain consistency and informs future
decisions.

20. Post-Launch Analysis:

- After your game's launch, perform post-mortem analysis to assess the effect
iveness of your data-driven decisions. Learn from both successes and failures
.

In conclusion, implementing data-driven decisions in game design is a powerful approach
to creating games that resonate with players and achieve your objectives. By collecting and
analyzing player data, conducting A/B tests, integrating feedback, and embracing an
iterative design process, you can continuously improve your game and adapt to player
preferences. Remember that data should enhance the player experience while maintaining
ethical standards and player privacy.

Section 14.4: Using Big Data for Predictive Modeling

Big data has become a game-changer in the field of game development, offering new possibilities for predictive modeling, personalization, and player engagement. In this section, we will explore how to harness the power of big data for predictive modeling in game design.

1. Data Aggregation:

- To start with predictive modeling, you need access to large datasets. This data can include player behavior, in-game actions, social interactions, and more. Modern game engines and analytics platforms facilitate data aggregation.

2. Data Cleaning and Preprocessing:

- Raw data is often messy and contains noise. Data cleaning and preprocessing are essential to ensure the accuracy and reliability of your predictive models. This involves handling missing values, outliers, and data transformation.

3. Feature Engineering:

- Feature engineering is the process of selecting, creating, or transforming features (variables) from your dataset that are relevant for predictive modeling. These features should capture aspects of player behavior or game dynamics that are important for your objectives.

4. Selecting Algorithms:

- Choose appropriate machine learning or data mining algorithms for your predictive modeling tasks. Common algorithms include decision trees, random forests, neural networks, and support vector machines. The choice depends on the nature of your data and objectives.

5. Predictive Objectives:

- Define clear predictive objectives. For example, you may want to predict player churn (when players stop playing), in-game purchases, or player progression through levels.

6. Model Training:

- Split your data into training and testing sets to train and evaluate your predictive models. Utilize cross-validation techniques to ensure robustness and accuracy.

7. Feature Importance:

- Assess feature importance to understand which variables have the most significant impact on your predictive objectives. This insight can guide game design decisions.

8. Predictive Analytics Tools:

- Employ specialized predictive analytics tools and libraries, such as scikit-learn (Python), TensorFlow, or PyTorch, to implement and train your predictive models.

9. Real-Time Predictions:

- In some cases, real-time predictions are necessary for personalized player experiences. Implement models that can make predictions during gameplay, such as suggesting personalized content or challenges.

10. Personalization:

- Leverage predictive modeling for player personalization. This can include recommending in-game items, difficulty adjustments, or story branches based on predicted player preferences.

11. Dynamic Difficulty Adjustment (DDA):

- Implement DDA systems that adapt the game's difficulty in real-time based on player performance and behavior. Predictive models can inform DDA decisions.

12. Retention and Engagement:

- Predictive modeling can help identify players at risk of churn and trigger retention strategies. Additionally, it can guide the design of engaging content and events.

13. Monetization Strategies:

- Optimize monetization strategies by predicting player spending behavior. This can involve recommending personalized in-game purchases or discounts.

14. Fairness and Bias:

- Be mindful of fairness and bias in predictive models. Ensure that your models do not discriminate against certain player groups and regularly evaluate model performance across diverse player segments.

15. Interpretability:

- Strive for model interpretability, especially when using machine learning techniques like neural networks. Understanding how and why models make predictions is crucial for refining game design decisions.

16. Continuous Improvement:

- Predictive models are not static; they should continuously adapt to changing player behavior and game dynamics. Regularly retrain and refine your models as new data becomes available.

17. Data Security and Privacy:

- Handle player data with utmost care, ensuring data security and privacy com
pliance. Transparency in data usage builds player trust.

18. Evaluation Metrics:

- Define appropriate evaluation metrics to measure the performance of your pr
edictive models. Common metrics include accuracy, precision, recall, and F1 s
core.

19. Ethical Considerations:

- Predictive modeling should be used responsibly. Avoid exploiting player vul
nerabilities or engaging in manipulative practices.

20. Player-First Approach:

- Always prioritize the player experience. Predictive modeling should enhance
enjoyment, personalization, and engagement without compromising player satisf
action.

In conclusion, big data and predictive modeling offer exciting opportunities for game design. By aggregating, cleaning, and preprocessing data, selecting suitable algorithms, defining clear objectives, and utilizing specialized tools, you can create predictive models that enhance player experiences, drive engagement, and inform game design decisions. However, ethical considerations, data privacy, and fairness should remain at the forefront of your predictive modeling endeavors to ensure responsible and player-centric game development.

Section 14.5: Ethical Considerations in Data Usage

As game developers increasingly leverage big data and analytics to enhance player experiences, it's vital to address the ethical considerations associated with data usage. Ethical game development not only fosters player trust but also aligns with industry standards and legal regulations. In this section, we'll explore the ethical aspects of using data in game development.

1. Informed Consent:

- Players should be informed about data collection practices and provide explicit consent. Transparency in privacy policies and user agreements is crucial. Explain what data is collected, how it will be used, and how players can opt out.

2. Data Minimization:

- Collect only the data necessary for improving gameplay or personalization. Avoid unnecessary data collection that might invade players' privacy.

3. Anonymization and Pseudonymization:

- Anonymize or pseudonymize player data to protect their identities. Remove personally identifiable information (PII) whenever possible.

4. Data Security:

- Implement robust data security measures to safeguard player information. Encrypt sensitive data and regularly update security protocols to prevent data breaches.

5. Retention Policies:

- Define data retention policies that specify how long player data will be stored. Avoid indefinite data retention unless legally required.

6. Consent Revocation:

- Allow players to revoke their consent for data collection and request the deletion of their data. Ensure a straightforward process for opting out.

7. Profiling and Targeting:

- Be cautious when using player data for profiling and targeted marketing. Avoid manipulating players or exploiting their vulnerabilities.

8. Fairness and Bias:

- Regularly evaluate algorithms for fairness and bias. Ensure that predictive models and algorithms do not discriminate against specific player groups, and address biases when identified.

9. Data Sharing and Third Parties:

- If sharing player data with third parties, obtain player consent and clearly communicate the purpose of data sharing. Ensure third parties comply with ethical data practices.

10. Children's Data:

- Comply with regulations like COPPA (Children's Online Privacy Protection Act) when dealing with data from players under the age of 13. Obtain parental consent when required.

11. Data Usage Transparency:

- Inform players how their data is being used to enhance their gaming experience. Be transparent about personalization, matchmaking, or content recommendations based on their data.

12. Data for Game Improvement:

- Use player data primarily for improving the game and enhancing player experiences, not for intrusive or manipulative purposes.

13. Cultural Sensitivity:

- Be culturally sensitive when collecting and using data from diverse player populations. Avoid actions that might be offensive or inappropriate in different cultural contexts.

14. Accessibility:

- Ensure that data-driven features, such as personalization, do not hinder accessibility for players with disabilities. Consider diverse player needs.

15. Regular Auditing:

- Conduct regular audits of data practices to ensure compliance with ethical standards and evolving regulations.

16. Responsible Data Science:

- Train data science teams and developers in responsible data usage practices. Foster a culture of ethics and data responsibility within your development studio.

17. Player Rights:

- Respect player rights to access their data, correct inaccuracies, and request data deletion. Provide clear mechanisms for players to exercise these rights.

18. Ethical Oversight:

- Establish an ethical oversight committee or individual within your organization to monitor data practices and address ethical concerns.

19. Community Engagement:

- Engage with your player community on data-related matters. Consider their feedback and concerns when making decisions about data usage.

20. Ethical Game Design:

- Ultimately, ethical data usage should align with ethical game design. Prioritize player well-being, enjoyment, and fairness in all aspects of your game.

Ethical considerations in data usage are pivotal in today's game development landscape. By upholding ethical standards, you not only build trust with players but also contribute to a responsible and player-centric gaming industry. Keep in mind that ethical data practices are an ongoing commitment that requires continuous monitoring and adaptation to evolving regulations and player expectations.

Chapter 15: Advanced Marketing and Community Building

Section 15.1: Strategic Marketing for High-End Games

In the highly competitive gaming industry, strategic marketing plays a pivotal role in the success of high-end games. Developing an exceptional game is just the first step; effectively promoting it to the right audience is equally crucial. This section delves into the strategies and tactics involved in marketing high-end games to ensure they reach their full potential.

1. Market Research and Analysis:

- Before launching your marketing campaign, conduct thorough market research. Understand your target audience, competitors, and industry trends. This data will inform your marketing strategy.

2. Unique Selling Proposition (USP):

- Define what sets your high-end game apart from others. Highlight its unique features and benefits. Your USP should resonate with your target audience.

3. Branding and Identity:

- Create a strong brand identity for your game. Develop a compelling logo, color scheme, and visual style that aligns with your game's theme. Consistent branding helps in recognition.

4. Pre-launch Hype:

- Generate excitement before the game's launch. Use teaser trailers, sneak peeks, and social media teasers to build anticipation. Engage with potential players early on.

5. Comprehensive Website:

- Develop a professional and informative website for your game. Include gameplay videos, screenshots, developer diaries, and press releases. Make it a hub for all game-related information.

6. Social Media Presence:

- Utilize social media platforms like Twitter, Facebook, Instagram, and YouTube to connect with your audience. Regularly post updates, interact with followers, and run contests or giveaways.

7. Influencer Marketing:

- Collaborate with gaming influencers and content creators. Their reviews and gameplay videos can have a significant impact on your game's visibility.

8. Community Engagement:

- Build a dedicated player community through forums, Discord, and Reddit. Listen to player feedback, address concerns, and involve the community in the development process.

9. Public Relations (PR):

- Reach out to gaming news outlets and bloggers for game reviews and coverage. Develop press kits with assets and information that make it easy for journalists to cover your game.

10. Email Marketing:

- Maintain an email list of interested players and potential customers. Send newsletters with updates, exclusive content, and special offers to keep them engaged.

11. Events and Conferences:

- Attend gaming events, conferences, and expos to showcase your game. It's an opportunity to network with industry professionals and gain exposure.

12. Demo Versions:

- Release demo versions of your game to let players experience it firsthand. Demos can build excitement and word-of-mouth promotion.

13. Paid Advertising:

- Invest in paid advertising campaigns on platforms like Google Ads, Facebook Ads, or Twitch Ads. Target specific demographics and monitor the campaign's performance.

14. Launch Strategy:

- Plan your game's launch meticulously. Choose the right release date, considering factors like competition and player expectations.

15. Post-launch Support:

- Continue to engage with your player community even after the game's release. Provide updates, fix bugs, and introduce new content to maintain player interest.

16. Reviews and Feedback:

- Encourage players to leave reviews on platforms like Steam or the App Store. Positive reviews and high ratings can boost your game's visibility.

17. Data Analytics:

- Use analytics tools to track the effectiveness of your marketing efforts. Adjust your strategy based on data-driven insights.

18. International Markets:

- Consider localization and international marketing strategies to expand your game's reach to global audiences.

19. User-Generated Content (UGC):

- Encourage players to create UGC, such as fan art, videos, or mods. UGC can amplify your game's visibility.

20. Long-term Strategy:

- Think beyond the initial launch. Develop a long-term marketing and community-building strategy to keep your game relevant and engaging over time.

Successful marketing for high-end games requires a combination of creativity, data-driven decision-making, and a deep understanding of the gaming community. By implementing these strategies and adapting to the ever-changing landscape of the gaming industry, you can maximize the visibility and success of your high-end game.

Section 15.2: Building and Nurturing an Online Community

Building and nurturing an online community is a fundamental aspect of successful game marketing and community engagement. An active and passionate player community can significantly impact a game's popularity, longevity, and overall success. In this section, we'll explore strategies for creating and maintaining a thriving online community around your high-end game.

1. Establish Official Channels:

- Start by creating official channels where players can gather and interact. This includes forums, social media pages, and dedicated community websites. Make these channels easily accessible from your game's website.

2. Community Guidelines:

- Establish clear community guidelines to maintain a positive and respectful atmosphere. Encourage constructive discussions and outline consequences for disruptive behavior.

3. Community Managers:

- Appoint dedicated community managers or moderators to oversee discussions, answer questions, and address concerns. They act as a bridge between the community and the development team.

4. Regular Updates:

- Keep the community engaged with regular updates. Share development progress, upcoming features, and behind-the-scenes insights. Transparency builds trust and excitement.

5. Developer Interaction:

- Foster a direct connection between developers and the community. Developers participating in discussions, hosting Q&A sessions, or sharing their experiences can create a sense of involvement and appreciation.

6. User-Generated Content (UGC):

- Encourage players to create UGC related to your game. Highlight fan art, videos, mods, and other player creations on your official channels. This shows appreciation for the community's contributions.

7. Events and Contests:

- Organize community events, contests, and challenges. These can range from in-game competitions to creative contests. Prizes or recognition can motivate participation.

8. Community Feedback:

- Actively seek and value community feedback. Implement player suggestions when possible, and communicate the changes made based on community input.

9. Developer Diaries:

- Share developer diaries or blog posts that delve into the game's development process. Discuss challenges, successes, and the creative decisions behind the game.

10. Exclusive Content:

- Offer exclusive content, such as early access, special in-game items, or be hind-the-scenes content, to community members who actively participate and co ntribute.

11. Livestreams and Podcasts:

- Host livestreams or podcasts featuring developers and community members. Th ese interactive sessions allow for direct communication and discussion.

12. Fan Clubs and Guilds:

- Encourage the formation of fan clubs or in-game guilds. These groups can or ganize events and activities, fostering a sense of camaraderie among players.

13. Patch Notes and Changelogs:

- Provide comprehensive patch notes and changelogs with each game update. Tra nsparency regarding changes and improvements demonstrates commitment to the c ommunity.

14. Player Spotlight:

- Spotlight exceptional players, content creators, or community members regularly. Highlighting their achievements and contributions can motivate others.

15. Surveys and Polls:

- Conduct surveys and polls to gather community opinions on various aspects of the game. Use the data to make informed decisions.

16. Celebrate Milestones:

- Celebrate significant community milestones, such as reaching a certain number of members or a game's anniversary. Throw virtual parties or offer in-game rewards.

17. Accessibility:

- Ensure that your community channels are accessible to as many players as possible. Consider language options, accessibility features, and different time zones.

18. Consistency:

- Maintain a consistent presence on your community channels. Regular updates and engagement show that you're invested in the community's well-being.

19. Conflict Resolution:

- Have a clear process for addressing conflicts within the community. Handling disputes promptly and fairly helps maintain a positive atmosphere.

20. Adapt and Evolve:

- Be open to adapting your community strategies based on the changing needs and preferences of your player base. Communities evolve, and so should your approach.

Nurturing an online community around your high-end game is an ongoing effort that requires dedication, communication, and a genuine interest in your players' experiences. When done effectively, it can result in a passionate and loyal player base that continues to support your game long after its release.

Section 15.3: Crowdfunding and Advanced Funding Strategies

Crowdfunding has become a popular way for game developers to secure funding for their high-end games while also engaging with the gaming community. In this section, we'll explore the world of crowdfunding and discuss advanced funding strategies that can help make your crowdfunding campaign a success.

1. Crowdfunding Basics:

- Crowdfunding platforms like Kickstarter, Indiegogo, and Fig allow developers to pitch their game ideas to the public. Backers pledge money in exchange for rewards or early access to the game.

2. Campaign Planning:

- A successful crowdfunding campaign starts with thorough planning. Define your goals, set a realistic funding target, and create compelling rewards for backers.

3. Showcase Your Vision:

- Craft a compelling and visually appealing campaign page that clearly communicates your game's vision. Include concept art, gameplay footage, and a well-written description.

4. Engage with Backers:

- Actively engage with your backers throughout the campaign. Respond to comments, answer questions, and provide updates to keep them excited.

5. Early Bird Rewards:

- Offer limited early bird rewards to incentivize backers to pledge quickly. These can include discounted copies of the game or exclusive in-game items.

6. Stretch Goals:

- Create stretch goals to encourage backers to increase their pledges. These are additional features or content that will be added to the game if funding surpasses the initial goal.

7. Marketing and Promotion:

- Promote your campaign through social media, gaming forums, and press releases. Partner with influencers and gaming media to reach a wider audience.

8. Demo or Prototype:

- Providing a playable demo or prototype can significantly boost your campaign's credibility. It allows backers to experience a portion of the game before pledging.

9. Regular Updates:

- Keep backers informed with regular updates. Share development progress, new features, and behind-the-scenes content to maintain excitement.

10. Backer Feedback:

- Listen to feedback from your backers and be willing to make adjustments to your game based on their suggestions. It demonstrates a commitment to delivering a great experience.

11. Transparency:

- Be transparent about how you'll use the funds. Break down the budget and explain where the money will go, such as development, marketing, and rewards fulfillment.

12. Post-Campaign Support:

- The relationship with backers doesn't end with the campaign's success. Keep them informed during development and provide post-campaign support.

13. Crowdfunding Platforms:

- Choose the right crowdfunding platform for your campaign. Each platform has its own rules, fees, and audience. Research which one aligns best with your project.

14. Legal Considerations:

- Understand the legal obligations of running a crowdfunding campaign. This includes delivering on promised rewards and complying with platform rules.

15. Alternative Funding Sources:

- Explore alternative funding sources, such as equity crowdfunding or partnerships with publishers, to supplement your crowdfunding efforts.

16. Learn from Others:

- Study successful crowdfunding campaigns in the gaming industry. Analyze what worked for them and adapt those strategies to your campaign.

17. Campaign Length:

- Choose an appropriate campaign length. Longer campaigns can lead to campaign fatigue, while shorter ones may not allow enough time to build momentum.

18. Post-Campaign Communication:

- After the campaign ends, continue to communicate with backers about the game's progress, expected release dates, and any delays.

19. Fulfilling Rewards:

- Ensure you have a plan in place to fulfill backer rewards promptly. Delays in reward delivery can lead to dissatisfaction among backers.

20. Thank Your Backers:

- Show appreciation to your backers for their support. Personalized thank-you messages or in-game acknowledgments can go a long way.

Crowdfunding can be a powerful way to finance your high-end game while building a dedicated community of supporters. By carefully planning your campaign, engaging with backers, and delivering on your promises, you can use crowdfunding as a stepping stone to bring your vision to life.

Section 15.4: Influencer Marketing and Public Relations

Influencer marketing and effective public relations (PR) strategies are critical components of a game developer's marketing arsenal. They can help increase your game's visibility, build anticipation, and create a positive buzz within the gaming community. In this section, we'll delve into the world of influencer marketing and PR, exploring how to harness their power to promote your high-end game effectively.

1. Identifying Influencers:

- Start by identifying influencers who align with your game's genre, style, and target audience. Research gaming YouTubers, Twitch streamers, bloggers, and social media personalities.

2. Building Relationships:

- Approach influencers professionally and build genuine relationships. Engage with their content, share their work, and reach out through email or social media to introduce yourself.

3. Providing Early Access:

- Offer influencers early access to your game. Allowing them to play and review it before release can generate excitement and provide valuable feedback.

4. Clear Guidelines:

- Establish clear guidelines for influencers regarding the content they create. Ensure they disclose any sponsorships and follow your game's branding and messaging.

5. Authenticity Matters:

- Encourage influencers to be authentic in their reviews and playthroughs. Audiences value genuine opinions over promotional content.

6. Diversify Platforms:

- Collaborate with influencers across various platforms, including YouTube, Twitch, Instagram, and Twitter. Each platform has its unique audience and reach.

7. PR Outreach:

- Develop a PR strategy that includes reaching out to gaming journalists, bloggers, and media outlets. Craft compelling press releases and game announcements.

8. Press Kits:

- Create comprehensive press kits with high-quality assets, including screenshots, gameplay videos, concept art, and a press release. Make them easily accessible on your website.

9. Pitching Your Story:

- When reaching out to journalists and bloggers, pitch your game's unique story, features, and what sets it apart from others in the genre.

10. Media Coverage:

- Secure media coverage in gaming publications, websites, and magazines. Positive reviews, interviews, and articles can help boost your game's credibility

11. Timing Matters:

- Consider the timing of your PR efforts. Plan announcements and releases strategically to maximize their impact.

12. Social Media Engagement:

- Leverage your social media channels to engage with your community and amplify your PR efforts. Share articles, reviews, and announcements.

13. Influencer Collaborations:

- Collaborate with influencers as part of your PR strategy. Their endorsement can reach a wider audience than traditional media.

14. Game Demos and Events:

- Showcase your game at gaming events, conventions, and expos. Offer demos to attendees and arrange interviews with influencers and journalists.

15. Responding to Feedback:

- Monitor feedback from influencers and the gaming community. Be prepared to address concerns and provide updates based on feedback.

16. Crisis Management:

- Develop a crisis management plan to handle any negative publicity or unexpected issues promptly and professionally.

17. Long-Term Relationships:

- Build long-term relationships with influencers and media outlets. Continuously nurture these connections for future projects.

18. Analytics and Tracking:

- Use analytics tools to measure the impact of your influencer marketing and PR efforts. Track website traffic, social media engagement, and game sales.

19. Budget Allocation:

- Allocate a portion of your marketing budget to influencer collaborations and PR activities. It's an investment in your game's success.

20. Adapt and Evolve:

- Stay adaptable and open to evolving your influencer marketing and PR strategies based on changing trends and audience preferences.

Influencer marketing and PR are essential tools in your game marketing toolkit. When executed effectively, they can help generate excitement, increase pre-release awareness, and ultimately contribute to the success of your high-end game. Building strong relationships with influencers and media outlets is an ongoing process that can yield significant returns in the long run.

Section 15.5: Post-Launch Support and Community Engagement

The launch of your high-end game is just the beginning of its journey in the gaming ecosystem. To maintain its success and longevity, you must invest in post-launch support and community engagement. In this section, we'll explore the importance of ongoing support and strategies for keeping your community engaged long after your game's release.

1. Patching and Updates:

- Regularly release patches and updates to address bugs, balance issues, and add new content. Transparently communicate these changes to your community through patch notes.

2. Active Community Management:

- Employ dedicated community managers to interact with players on forums, social media, and other platforms. Address their concerns, gather feedback, and foster a positive environment.

3. Player Feedback:

- Encourage players to share their feedback and suggestions. Implementing player-driven changes can improve the game's overall experience and demonstrate your commitment to the community.

4. Expansions and DLCs:

- Plan and develop expansions or downloadable content (DLC) to keep players engaged and excited about your game. These additions can introduce new features, storylines, or gameplay elements.

5. Live Events and Challenges:

- Organize in-game events, challenges, or competitions to keep players invested in your game. Offer unique rewards or recognition for participation.

6. Communication Channels:

- Maintain a strong online presence through official websites, social media, and community forums. Keep players informed about upcoming content, events, and news related to your game.

7. Player Support:

- Provide reliable player support to assist users with technical issues and inquiries. A responsive support team can enhance the player experience.

8. Transparency and Honesty:

- Be transparent about your game's development, challenges, and future plans. Honesty builds trust and rapport with the community.

9. Developer Q&A Sessions:

- Host regular developer Q&A sessions or livestreams to connect with your player base. Answer their questions, discuss game updates, and share insights into your development process.

10. Community Feedback Panels:

- Establish community feedback panels or focus groups to involve dedicated players in the decision-making process for future updates and features.

11. User-Generated Content:

- Encourage and support user-generated content (UGC) creation, such as mods, skins, or custom levels. Highlight outstanding UGC contributions.

12. Monetization Strategies:

- Implement fair and balanced monetization strategies for in-game purchases, if applicable. Avoid pay-to-win models and prioritize cosmetic items.

13. Celebrate Milestones:

- Celebrate game milestones, anniversaries, and achievements with the community. Consider offering exclusive rewards or events during these occasions.

14. Cross-Platform Play:

- If feasible, enable cross-platform play to unite players across different gaming platforms, fostering a larger and more active player base.

15. User Surveys:

- Conduct periodic user surveys to gather insights and preferences directly from your player community. Use the data to guide future development decisions.

16. Community Spotlights:

- Showcase community-created content, fan art, and fan fiction to celebrate your players' contributions to the game's ecosystem.

17. Listen and Adapt:

- Continuously listen to your community's needs and adapt your post-launch strategy accordingly. Flexibility and responsiveness are key.

18. Maintain Game Servers:

- Ensure the stability and performance of game servers, minimizing downtime and disruptions for players.

19. Manage Toxicity:

- Implement measures to address toxicity and harassment within your game's community. A welcoming and respectful environment encourages player retention.

20. Long-Term Vision:

- Maintain a long-term vision for your game's development, even after the initial excitement wanes. Cultivate a loyal player base that can sustain your game's success for years to come.

Post-launch support and community engagement are vital for maintaining the health and longevity of your high-end game. By actively nurturing your player community, addressing their needs, and continually improving the game, you can create a lasting and successful gaming experience that stands the test of time.

Chapter 16: CryEngine in the Professional Sphere

Section 16.1: Using CryEngine in AAA Game Development

CryEngine has earned its place in the professional game development sphere as a robust and versatile engine capable of delivering high-quality experiences. In this section, we'll explore how CryEngine is leveraged in AAA game development, where the demands for performance, graphics, and gameplay reach their zenith.

The Appeal of CryEngine for AAA Titles

AAA game development focuses on creating blockbuster titles that push the boundaries of technology and storytelling. CryEngine's strengths lie in its cutting-edge graphical capabilities, realistic physics, and extensive toolset, making it an attractive choice for developers aiming to deliver top-tier gaming experiences.

CryEngine's real-time rendering prowess allows for stunning visuals, from lifelike character models to breathtaking environments. This engine's versatility enables developers to craft diverse game worlds, whether it's an open-world adventure, a sci-fi epic, or a historical simulation.

Collaboration and Team Dynamics

AAA game development involves large teams of artists, programmers, designers, and writers working in unison to bring a game to life. CryEngine facilitates collaboration through its robust project management and version control features. Teams can seamlessly integrate their assets, code, and design elements, ensuring a cohesive development process.

Managing Large-Scale Projects

Managing the scope and scale of AAA projects can be daunting. CryEngine provides tools for project management, asset tracking, and content creation that streamline the development pipeline. Additionally, its modular architecture allows for the creation of custom workflows tailored to the specific needs of a project.

Industry Standards and Best Practices

In the AAA game development realm, adherence to industry standards and best practices is crucial. CryEngine ensures compliance with industry standards and offers guidelines for optimizing performance and maintaining quality throughout development. This includes recommendations for efficient memory management, code optimization, and platform-specific optimizations.

Networking and Professional Development

Networking is an essential aspect of AAA game development. CryEngine fosters connections within the industry by providing resources for developers to collaborate, learn, and share knowledge. Conferences, forums, and workshops related to CryEngine offer opportunities for professional growth and networking.

Conclusion

Using CryEngine in AAA game development offers a powerful platform for realizing ambitious projects. Its advanced capabilities, collaborative features, and adherence to industry standards make it a go-to choice for developers seeking to create groundbreaking and immersive gaming experiences. In the following sections, we will delve deeper into the intricacies of managing large-scale projects, implementing industry best practices, and navigating the professional landscape of game development.

Section 16.2: Collaboration and Team Management Tools

Collaboration and effective team management are essential components of successful AAA game development when utilizing CryEngine. In this section, we will delve into the tools and strategies that empower development teams to work together seamlessly and efficiently.

Version Control Systems

Version control systems (VCS) play a pivotal role in maintaining the integrity of a game project. CryEngine is compatible with popular VCS solutions such as Git, Mercurial, and Perforce. These systems allow team members to track changes to the project's code, assets, and resources. By keeping a history of revisions, VCS enables developers to roll back to previous states, compare changes, and resolve conflicts. This ensures that the project remains stable and that multiple team members can work on different parts of the game simultaneously.

Asset Management

Effective asset management is crucial for organizing and sharing resources within the development team. CryEngine provides tools for managing and categorizing game assets, including 3D models, textures, audio files, and scripts. Assets are stored in a structured hierarchy, making it easy for team members to access and use them in their work. The engine's asset pipeline also supports automatic conversion and optimization, reducing the manual workload on artists and designers.

Project Collaboration

CryEngine includes features that facilitate project collaboration. Teams can create and share project templates, allowing for standardized setups and workflows. The engine's project management tools enable teams to define roles and responsibilities for team members, ensuring clarity in the development process. Additionally, project documentation and task tracking can be integrated directly into the engine, making it easier to keep everyone on the same page.

Script Collaboration

In CryEngine, scripting plays a vital role in defining gameplay mechanics and interactions. CryScript, a proprietary scripting language, allows developers to write custom code to extend and enhance the engine's functionality. Collaboration on scripts is made more straightforward with built-in code editors, code validation tools, and debugging support. CryEngine also supports external code editors, enabling developers to work with their preferred coding environment.

Remote Collaboration

Modern game development often involves team members working remotely from different locations. CryEngine offers remote collaboration capabilities through cloud-based asset storage and project sharing. Team members can access the project and its assets from anywhere with an internet connection, making it easier to maintain productivity and ensure that the development process remains efficient, even in remote or distributed team setups.

Conclusion

Collaboration and team management are critical aspects of AAA game development with CryEngine. Effective utilization of version control systems, asset management tools, and project collaboration features ensures that the development process remains organized and streamlined. As teams work together to bring ambitious game projects to life, CryEngine's comprehensive suite of collaboration tools plays a pivotal role in their success. In the subsequent sections, we will explore more aspects of managing large-scale projects, adhering to industry standards, and navigating the professional landscape of AAA game development.

Section 16.3: Managing Large-Scale Projects in CryEngine

Managing large-scale game development projects in CryEngine requires careful planning, coordination, and adherence to industry best practices. In this section, we will explore the strategies and considerations that game development teams should keep in mind when working on ambitious projects with the CryEngine.

Project Scope and Planning

One of the first and most critical steps in managing a large-scale project is defining its scope. This includes determining the game's features, mechanics, art style, and overall design. A well-defined scope serves as a roadmap for the project and helps prevent scope creep, which can lead to delays and budget overruns.

CryEngine provides project management tools that allow teams to create detailed project plans, define milestones, and allocate resources effectively. Project managers can set clear goals and timelines, making it easier to track progress and ensure that the project stays on course.

Team Organization and Roles

In a large-scale game development project, it's essential to have a well-organized team with clearly defined roles and responsibilities. CryEngine offers features for role assignment and access control, ensuring that team members can access only the parts of the project relevant to their work.

Roles typically include game designers, level designers, artists, programmers, and quality assurance testers, among others. Effective team organization helps distribute the workload efficiently and ensures that each aspect of the game receives the attention it needs.

Version Control and Collaboration

Large teams working on complex projects require robust version control systems (VCS) to manage code, assets, and resources. CryEngine supports popular VCS solutions such as Git, Mercurial, and Perforce, allowing teams to track changes, resolve conflicts, and maintain code integrity.

Collaboration tools within CryEngine enable team members to work together seamlessly. These tools facilitate communication, asset sharing, and project documentation. They also ensure that everyone is on the same page, even when team members are working remotely or from different locations.

Asset Management and Optimization

Efficient asset management is crucial in large-scale projects, where the volume of 3D models, textures, audio files, and scripts can be substantial. CryEngine's asset management tools help organize assets, automate conversion, and optimize resources to improve performance.

Artists and designers can use CryEngine's built-in tools to create and import assets directly into the engine. These tools support various asset formats, making it easier to work with external software packages commonly used in the industry.

Quality Assurance and Testing

Large-scale projects often require rigorous quality assurance (QA) and testing processes. CryEngine offers debugging and profiling tools to help identify and resolve issues promptly. Automated testing, including performance testing and bug tracking, can be integrated into the development pipeline.

Quality assurance teams can use CryEngine's built-in testing features to simulate gameplay scenarios, test AI behavior, and ensure the game's stability and performance. This iterative testing process is vital in identifying and addressing issues early in development.

Scaling for Multiplatform

Many large-scale projects target multiple platforms, including PC, consoles, and potentially mobile devices. CryEngine's multiplatform support allows developers to build and optimize their games for various hardware configurations and operating systems.

Scaling for different platforms involves adapting graphics settings, input methods, and performance optimizations. CryEngine provides tools and documentation to help developers ensure their games run smoothly and consistently across different platforms.

Conclusion

Managing large-scale game development projects in CryEngine requires a combination of careful planning, effective team organization, and the utilization of the engine's robust features. By defining project scope, organizing teams, implementing version control, optimizing assets, conducting quality assurance, and scaling for multiplatform releases, development teams can navigate the challenges of large-scale projects successfully. In the next section, we will delve into industry standards and best practices that are crucial for delivering high-quality games with CryEngine.

Section 16.4: Industry Standards and Best Practices

In the world of game development, adhering to industry standards and best practices is essential for creating successful and high-quality games. When working with CryEngine, developers should keep these standards in mind to ensure their projects are well-received by players and meet industry expectations.

1. Coding Conventions and Style Guidelines

Maintaining consistent coding conventions and style guidelines is crucial for code readability and maintainability. CryEngine provides its own coding standards, which developers should follow to ensure code uniformity. This includes naming conventions, commenting practices, and code structure. Adhering to these standards helps team members understand and work with each other's code more efficiently.

```
// Example of CryEngine's naming convention
void OnUpdate(float deltaTime) {
    // Function body
}
```

2. Performance Optimization

Optimizing game performance is paramount, especially in large-scale projects. CryEngine offers profiling tools that assist in identifying performance bottlenecks. Developers should profile their games regularly and use optimization techniques such as efficient rendering, memory management, and multithreading to ensure smooth gameplay experiences.

```
-- Example of optimizing AI behavior
function OptimizeAI(aiEntity)
    -- AI optimization code here
end
```

3. Cross-Platform Compatibility

To reach a broader audience, many games are developed for multiple platforms. CryEngine supports cross-platform development, but developers must ensure their games run smoothly on each target platform. This includes adapting controls, graphics settings, and performance optimizations specific to each platform.

```
-- Example of cross-platform input handling
if platform == "PC" then
    -- PC input handling
elseif platform == "Console" then
    -- Console input handling
end
```

4. Accessibility and Inclusivity

Game accessibility and inclusivity have gained increasing importance in recent years. Developers should follow accessibility guidelines to ensure their games are playable by a diverse audience, including individuals with disabilities. This includes options for subtitles, customizable controls, and considerations for colorblind players.

```
// Example of adding accessibility features
if (isColorBlindModeEnabled) {
    // Adjust game visuals for colorblind players
}
```

5. Security and Player Privacy

Protecting player data and ensuring online security is a top priority. When implementing online features or handling user information, developers should follow best practices for data encryption, secure authentication, and player privacy. This helps prevent data breaches and maintains player trust.

```
// Example of secure player data handling
if (isUserLoggedIn) {
    // Perform secure operations with user data
}
```

6. Documentation and Knowledge Sharing

Comprehensive documentation is essential for project continuity and knowledge sharing among team members. Developers should maintain up-to-date documentation that covers code, assets, design decisions, and project guidelines. This documentation streamlines onboarding for new team members and aids in troubleshooting.

Game Design Document

- Overview
- Gameplay Mechanics
- Level Design
- Art Style
- Sound Design

7. Community Engagement and Feedback

Engaging with the player community and gathering feedback is a valuable practice. Developers should establish communication channels, such as forums or social media, where players can share their thoughts and report issues. This feedback loop helps identify improvements and build a dedicated player base.

Community Feedback Forum

- Bug Reports
- Suggestions for Enhancements
- Player Experiences
- General Discussions

Conclusion

Following industry standards and best practices when working with CryEngine is essential for achieving success in large-scale game development. By adhering to coding conventions, optimizing performance, ensuring cross-platform compatibility, prioritizing accessibility and security, maintaining documentation, and engaging with the player community, developers can create outstanding games that meet or exceed player expectations. In the next section, we will explore networking and professional development opportunities in the world of CryEngine game development.

Section 16.5: Networking and Professional Development

Networking and professional development are integral aspects of a successful career in game development, especially when working with a powerful engine like CryEngine. This section explores the significance of building connections within the industry and continuing to enhance one's skills and knowledge.

1. Industry Networking

Networking with fellow game developers, industry professionals, and potential collaborators can open doors to opportunities and knowledge sharing. Attending industry events, conferences, and game jams provides valuable chances to connect with others who share your passion. Online platforms like LinkedIn and game development forums also serve as excellent networking resources.

Upcoming Industry Events

- Game Developers Conference (GDC)
- E3 Expo
- Indie Game Developer Meetup
- Game Jams and Hackathons

2. Professional Associations and Organizations

Joining professional associations related to game development can provide access to resources, mentorship, and networking opportunities. Associations like the International Game Developers Association (IGDA) offer memberships, events, and forums where developers can learn, grow, and collaborate.

Professional Associations

- International Game Developers Association (IGDA)
- Entertainment Software Association (ESA)
- Women in Games International (WIGI)
- Indie Game Developers Association (IGDA)

3. Continuous Learning

The game development industry evolves rapidly, with new technologies and trends emerging regularly. Developers should commit to continuous learning by exploring online courses, tutorials, and workshops. Learning platforms like Udemy, Coursera, and Unity Learn offer courses on various aspects of game development.

Online Learning Platforms

- Udemy
- Coursera
- Pluralsight
- Unity Learn

4. Portfolio Development

Maintaining an impressive portfolio is crucial when seeking employment or freelance opportunities. Regularly update your portfolio with projects, code samples, and game demos that showcase your skills and creativity. A strong portfolio can significantly impact your career prospects.

Portfolio Components

- Game Projects
- Code Snippets
- Artwork and Assets
- Design Documents

5. Mentorship and Collaboration

Seeking mentorship from experienced professionals can accelerate your career growth. Additionally, collaborating on game projects with others allows you to learn from their expertise and develop teamwork skills. Mentorship programs and collaborative platforms like GitHub can facilitate these connections.

Mentorship Opportunities

- Mentorship Programs (IGDA Mentorship Program)
- Collaborative Platforms (GitHub)
- Game Development Workshops

6. Staying Informed

Keeping up with industry news and trends is essential. Subscribe to game development publications, follow game news websites, and join relevant online communities to stay informed. Knowledge of industry trends and emerging technologies can give you a competitive edge.

Industry News Sources

- Gamasutra
- GameSpot
- Kotaku
- Polygon

7. Contribute to Open Source

Contributing to open-source game development projects not only gives back to the community but also enhances your skills and visibility. Platforms like GitHub host numerous open-source game projects that welcome contributions and collaboration.

Open Source Game Projects

- Godot Engine
- 0 A.D. (Real-Time Strategy Game)
- Terasology (Minecraft-Inspired Game)
- Cataclysm: Dark Days Ahead (Survival Roguelike)

Conclusion

Networking and professional development are essential components of a successful career in game development. Building industry connections, joining professional associations, continuous learning, maintaining a strong portfolio, seeking mentorship, staying informed, and contributing to open-source projects all contribute to your growth and advancement in the field. These practices not only enhance your skills but also broaden your horizons in the world of CryEngine and game development. In the next chapter, we will explore emerging technologies and future directions in game development.

Chapter 17: Emerging Technologies and Future Directions

Section 17.1: Integrating Emerging Technologies with CryEngine

In the ever-evolving landscape of game development, staying at the forefront of emerging technologies is crucial. This section delves into how CryEngine can adapt and incorporate these innovations, ensuring its relevance in the future of the gaming industry.

1. Virtual Reality (VR) and Augmented Reality (AR)

VR and AR technologies have gained significant traction in recent years, providing immersive experiences beyond traditional gaming. CryEngine can embrace VR and AR by optimizing rendering pipelines, implementing intuitive VR interactions, and supporting AR experiences on mobile devices.

VR/AR Development Tools

- CryEngine VR and AR SDKs
- Integration with Oculus Rift, HTC Vive, HoloLens, and ARCore
- Designing for Mixed Reality (MR) Environments

2. Cloud Gaming and Streaming

The rise of cloud gaming platforms like Google Stadia and NVIDIA GeForce NOW presents new opportunities for CryEngine. Developers can explore seamless integration with these services, allowing players to enjoy high-quality CryEngine games on various devices without the need for powerful hardware.

Cloud Gaming Integration

- CryEngine Cloud SDK
- Leveraging Game Streaming APIs
- Optimizing for Low-Latency Streaming

3. Artificial Intelligence (AI) Advancements

AI is evolving rapidly, offering more realistic and adaptive behaviors for in-game characters. CryEngine can harness AI advancements by integrating machine learning algorithms, enhancing NPC interactions, and creating dynamic, AI-driven game worlds.

AI Integration

- Machine Learning Libraries (TensorFlow, PyTorch)
- AI Behavior Trees and Decision-Making Systems
- Adaptive AI Opponents in Multiplayer Games

4. Ray Tracing and Realistic Graphics

As hardware becomes more capable, real-time ray tracing and photorealistic graphics are becoming achievable in games. CryEngine can continue pushing the boundaries of visual fidelity by optimizing ray tracing implementations, enhancing global illumination, and delivering jaw-dropping visuals.

Graphics Advancements

- CryEngine Ray Tracing Engine
- Integration with NVIDIA RTX and AMD RDNA2 Features
- Real-Time Ray-Traced Reflections and Shadows

5. Blockchain and NFT Integration

The blockchain revolution has introduced new possibilities for ownership and monetization in gaming. CryEngine can explore integrating blockchain technology, enabling players to own in-game assets as NFTs (Non-Fungible Tokens) and trade them on blockchain marketplaces.

Blockchain Features

- CryEngine Blockchain SDK
- NFT Asset Creation and Management
- Secure and Transparent Asset Ownership

6. Environmental and Social Impact Considerations

As the gaming industry grows, so does its impact on the environment and society. CryEngine can lead by example in adopting sustainable development practices, reducing carbon footprints, and promoting diversity and inclusion within the industry.

Sustainability Initiatives

- Eco-Friendly Game Development Guidelines
- Inclusivity and Accessibility Features
- Ethical Game Monetization Strategies

Conclusion

The future of CryEngine lies in its ability to adapt to emerging technologies and embrace innovation. By integrating VR and AR, exploring cloud gaming, harnessing AI advancements, pushing the boundaries of graphics, adopting blockchain and NFTs, and considering environmental and social impacts, CryEngine can remain a cutting-edge game development engine in a rapidly evolving industry. This chapter has provided a glimpse into the potential future directions of CryEngine, setting the stage for the next generation of gaming experiences. In the following chapter, we will delve into career advancement and leadership in the game development field.

Section 17.2: Anticipating Future Trends in Game Development

To stay competitive in the game development industry, it's essential to anticipate and adapt to future trends. This section explores some key trends that may shape the future of game development and how CryEngine can position itself to leverage these trends effectively.

1. Metaverse and Persistent Worlds

The concept of the metaverse, a shared virtual space where users can interact and create, is gaining momentum. CryEngine can evolve to support the creation of metaverse-like experiences by providing tools for large-scale persistent worlds, user-generated content, and social interactions within the engine.

Metaverse Development

- Extending CryEngine's Networking Capabilities
- User-Generated Content Tools
- Seamless Cross-Platform Integration

2. Player-Driven Narratives

Players increasingly seek personalized and dynamic storytelling experiences. CryEngine can enhance its narrative capabilities by integrating AI-driven story generation, player choices, and consequences, allowing developers to create richer, more adaptive narratives.

Player-Driven Storytelling

- AI-Powered Narrative Generators
- Choice-Driven Narrative Systems
- Branching Story Structures

3. Haptic Feedback and Immersion

Advancements in haptic feedback technology offer the potential for deeper immersion. CryEngine can explore integration with haptic feedback devices, enabling players to feel the environment and in-game events more realistically.

Haptic Feedback Integration

- Support for Haptic Feedback Controllers (e.g., VR gloves)
- Enhanced Environmental Feedback
- Realistic Physically-Based Feedback Effects

4. Cross-Reality Experiences

Blending the physical and virtual worlds is an emerging trend. CryEngine can expand into augmented reality (AR) and mixed reality (MR) development, enabling developers to create games that seamlessly integrate with the real world.

Cross-Reality Development

- AR and MR Toolsets
- Integration with AR Glasses and Devices
- Location-Based Mixed Reality Games

5. Sustainability and Eco-Friendly Practices

As environmental concerns grow, CryEngine can lead by adopting eco-friendly development practices. This includes optimizing resource usage, reducing energy consumption, and encouraging developers to create environmentally conscious games.

Sustainability Initiatives

- Eco-Friendly Game Development Guidelines
- Energy-Efficient Rendering Techniques
- Carbon Footprint Monitoring Tools

6. Ethical AI and Inclusivity

Ethical considerations in AI development and inclusivity in gaming are becoming increasingly important. CryEngine can incorporate AI ethics guidelines and accessibility features to ensure games are inclusive and respectful of diverse player backgrounds.

Ethical AI and Inclusivity

- Ethical AI Development Frameworks
- Accessibility and Inclusive Design Practices
- Representation and Sensitivity Training for Developers

Conclusion

Anticipating and adapting to future trends in game development is crucial for the continued success of CryEngine. By considering the metaverse, player-driven narratives, haptic feedback, cross-reality experiences, sustainability, and ethical AI, CryEngine can position itself as a forward-thinking engine that empowers developers to create innovative and inclusive gaming experiences. This chapter has highlighted the potential future directions of CryEngine, setting the stage for its continued evolution in the dynamic world of game development. In the next chapter, we will delve into the role of CryEngine in future gaming ecosystems.

Section 17.3: CryEngine and the Next Generation of Gaming

The next generation of gaming promises exciting advancements in technology, gameplay, and player experiences. CryEngine, as a powerful game engine, plays a significant role in shaping this future. In this section, we will explore the key aspects of CryEngine's involvement in the next generation of gaming.

1. Cutting-Edge Graphics and Realism

Next-gen gaming demands visually stunning experiences, and CryEngine has always been at the forefront of graphics technology. With support for ray tracing, global illumination, and high-dynamic-range imaging (HDRI), CryEngine continues to deliver unparalleled realism in game visuals.

Graphics Advancements

- Ray Tracing Integration
- Realistic Global Illumination
- HDR Imaging Techniques

2. Seamless Cross-Platform Play

Cross-platform gaming is a growing trend, and CryEngine adapts by providing robust support for cross-device and cross-platform gameplay. Developers can create games that allow players on various platforms to interact seamlessly.

Cross-Platform Integration

- Multiplatform Network Synchronization
- Cross-Device Gameplay
- Shared Game Worlds Across Platforms

3. Advanced AI and Machine Learning

AI-driven experiences are becoming increasingly sophisticated. CryEngine's integration of advanced AI and machine learning tools empowers developers to create intelligent NPCs, adaptive gameplay, and procedurally generated content.

AI and ML Capabilities

- Advanced AI Behavior Trees
- Machine Learning for NPC Behavior
- AI-Generated Game Content

4. Accessibility and Inclusivity

The gaming community is diverse, and inclusivity is a priority. CryEngine enhances accessibility features, ensuring that games built on the engine are playable and enjoyable for a broad audience, including players with disabilities.

Inclusivity Initiatives

- Accessible User Interfaces
- Customizable Controls
- Support for Assistive Technologies

5. Real-Time Collaboration and Streaming

Collaborative game development and real-time streaming are essential for the future. CryEngine invests in tools that facilitate remote collaboration among developers and supports streaming platforms for live gameplay and content creation.

Collaboration and Streaming

- Real-Time Collaboration Tools
- Integration with Live Streaming Platforms
- Remote Game Development Workflows

6. Environmental Responsibility

As sustainability becomes a central concern, CryEngine promotes environmentally responsible development practices. This includes optimizing resource usage, reducing energy consumption, and raising awareness of ecological issues through games.

Environmental Sustainability

- Eco-Friendly Game Development Guidelines
- Energy-Efficient Rendering Techniques
- Promoting Environmental Awareness in Games

Conclusion

CryEngine's evolution is closely tied to the next generation of gaming. With its focus on cutting-edge graphics, cross-platform play, advanced AI, accessibility, real-time collaboration, and environmental responsibility, CryEngine is well-positioned to be a driving force in shaping the future of gaming. As the gaming industry continues to evolve, CryEngine remains at the forefront, empowering developers to create groundbreaking and immersive gaming experiences. In the following section, we will delve into the sustainability and environmental considerations within game development, addressing critical issues for the industry's future.

Section 17.4: Sustainability and Environmental Considerations

The gaming industry, like many others, is increasingly aware of its impact on the environment. As technology advances and games become more complex, it's crucial for developers and game engine providers to consider sustainability and environmental responsibility in their practices. CryEngine, as a leading game engine, is committed to addressing these concerns. In this section, we'll explore the sustainability and environmental considerations within game development and how CryEngine contributes to a greener gaming future.

1. Energy-Efficient Rendering Techniques

One significant aspect of sustainability is reducing energy consumption. CryEngine has been actively developing energy-efficient rendering techniques that maintain high-quality visuals while minimizing the hardware resources required. This approach ensures that games built on CryEngine are optimized for lower power consumption on gaming platforms.

Energy-Efficient Rendering

- Dynamic Resolution Scaling
- Adaptive Graphics Settings
- Efficient GPU and CPU Utilization

2. Eco-Friendly Game Development Guidelines

CryEngine provides guidelines for eco-friendly game development. This includes best practices for asset optimization, reducing unnecessary resource usage, and minimizing the environmental footprint of games. Developers are encouraged to follow these guidelines to create games that are both visually stunning and environmentally responsible.

Eco-Friendly Development

- Asset Optimization Tips
- Reducing Wasteful Resource Loading
- Minimizing Game's Carbon Footprint

3. Promoting Environmental Awareness in Games

Games have a unique ability to raise awareness about environmental issues. CryEngine supports developers in integrating eco-themed content and narratives into their games. This not only educates players about environmental challenges but also encourages them to take real-world actions.

Environmental Awareness

- Eco-Themed Game Storytelling
- Interactive Environmental Challenges
- Real-World Activism Integration

4. Recyclable Packaging and Distribution

CryEngine encourages sustainable practices in game distribution. Developers can explore options for eco-friendly packaging, digital distribution, and reduced physical waste. By minimizing the environmental impact of game packaging and distribution, CryEngine contributes to a greener gaming industry.

Sustainable Distribution

- Digital-First Distribution Models

- Eco-Friendly Packaging Options
- Reducing Physical Waste in Game Distribution

5. Carbon Offsetting and Environmental Partnerships

CryEngine is committed to offsetting its carbon footprint by investing in environmental initiatives. The engine provider also collaborates with environmental organizations and encourages developers to participate in similar initiatives, fostering a culture of environmental responsibility within the gaming community.

Carbon Offsetting and Partnerships

- Offset Engine-Related Carbon Emissions
- Collaborations with Environmental NGOs
- Encouraging Developer Involvement

Conclusion

Sustainability and environmental considerations are integral to the future of the gaming industry. CryEngine recognizes its role in shaping this future and is actively working to reduce energy consumption, promote eco-friendly development practices, raise environmental awareness through games, and minimize the environmental impact of game distribution. By embracing these principles, CryEngine contributes to a more sustainable and responsible gaming ecosystem. In the next chapter, we will explore career advancement and leadership opportunities in the game development industry, focusing on how individuals can make a positive impact while pursuing their careers.

Section 17.5: The Role of CryEngine in Future Gaming Ecosystems

As we look ahead to the future of gaming, it's evident that CryEngine will continue to play a significant role in shaping the gaming ecosystem. In this final section of the book, we'll explore the various ways in which CryEngine is positioned to influence and adapt to emerging trends, technologies, and challenges in the gaming industry.

1. Embracing Emerging Technologies

CryEngine has a strong track record of embracing emerging technologies such as virtual reality (VR), augmented reality (AR), and real-time ray tracing. In the coming years, as these technologies become more widespread, CryEngine will likely remain at the forefront of their integration into gaming experiences.

Adapting to Emerging Tech

- VR and AR Integration
- Real-Time Ray Tracing
- Compatibility with Future Hardware

2. Cross-Platform and Cross-Device Gaming

The gaming landscape is evolving with an increasing focus on cross-platform and cross-device gaming experiences. CryEngine's versatility and adaptability make it well-suited for creating games that can be seamlessly played across various platforms and devices, fostering a more inclusive gaming community.

Cross-Platform Gaming

- Multi-Device Gameplay
- Seamless Cross-Platform Integration
- Expanding Player Bases

3. Environmental Sustainability

CryEngine's commitment to environmental sustainability aligns with the broader trend of eco-consciousness in the gaming industry. As sustainability becomes a more significant concern, CryEngine will continue to develop features and practices that reduce the environmental impact of game development.

Green Game Development

- Energy-Efficient Rendering
- Eco-Friendly Development Guidelines
- Carbon Offsetting Initiatives

4. Community and Collaboration

The future of gaming is likely to be characterized by increased collaboration and community involvement. CryEngine fosters this trend by providing tools and resources that facilitate collaboration among developers, artists, and players, contributing to the growth of a vibrant gaming community.

Community-Centric Approach

- Collaborative Game Development
- Modding and Player-Created Content
- Active Community Engagement

5. Accessibility and Inclusivity

As the gaming audience diversifies, accessibility and inclusivity will remain paramount. CryEngine's dedication to inclusive design practices and customizable user interfaces ensures that games developed with the engine can cater to a broad range of players, including those with varying abilities and preferences.

Inclusive Gaming

- Customizable User Interfaces

- Accessibility Features
- Inclusive Gameplay Design

Conclusion

CryEngine's adaptability, commitment to emerging technologies, sustainability initiatives, support for cross-platform gaming, and emphasis on community and inclusivity position it as a key player in the future of gaming ecosystems. The engine's continued evolution and responsiveness to industry trends ensure that it will remain a vital tool for developers looking to create cutting-edge, environmentally responsible, and inclusive gaming experiences.

As we conclude this book, we hope it has provided valuable insights into the capabilities and potential of CryEngine. Whether you are a seasoned developer, an aspiring game creator, or simply someone interested in the world of game development, CryEngine offers exciting opportunities to explore, innovate, and shape the future of interactive entertainment. Thank you for joining us on this journey, and we wish you the best of luck in your endeavors in the dynamic and ever-evolving realm of game development.

Chapter 18: Career Advancement and Leadership in Game Development

Section 18.1: Advancing Your Career with CryEngine

In the competitive and rapidly evolving field of game development, advancing your career requires a combination of skills, dedication, and strategic decision-making. In this section, we will explore how CryEngine can be a valuable asset in advancing your career and how you can leverage its features and opportunities to stand out in the industry.

1. Building a Strong Portfolio

A portfolio showcasing your work is crucial for career advancement in game development. CryEngine's visually stunning capabilities make it an excellent choice for creating impressive game projects that can serve as the centerpiece of your portfolio.

Portfolio Development

- Showcasing CryEngine-Powered Projects
- Highlighting Technical and Artistic Skills
- Diversifying Project Types (e.g., games, simulations)

2. Networking and Collaboration

Game development is a collaborative field, and networking is essential. CryEngine's community and professional network offer opportunities to connect with other developers, artists, and industry professionals. Participating in forums, attending events, and collaborating on projects can expand your network and open doors to career opportunities.

Networking Strategies

- Active Participation in CryEngine Community
- Attending Game Development Conferences
- Joining Online Game Dev Communities

3. Learning and Skill Development

Continuously improving your skills and staying up-to-date with industry trends is crucial for career growth. CryEngine provides extensive documentation, tutorials, and resources to enhance your knowledge and capabilities.

Skill Enhancement

- Access to CryEngine Learning Resources
- Exploring Advanced Engine Features
- Keeping Up with Industry Best Practices

4. Career Paths in Game Development with CryEngine

CryEngine opens doors to various career paths within the game development industry, including roles such as game developer, level designer, 3D artist, technical artist, and more. Understanding your strengths and interests can help you choose the career path that aligns with your goals.

Career Path Options

- Game Developer
- Level Designer
- 3D Artist
- Technical Artist
- Game Programmer
- Game Producer

5. Entrepreneurship and Starting Your Own Studio

For those with entrepreneurial aspirations, CryEngine provides a platform to develop and publish your own games. Starting an indie game studio or pursuing solo game development projects is a viable path to career advancement in the industry.

Indie Game Development

- Developing and Publishing Indie Games
- Navigating Challenges as an Independent Developer
- Marketing and Distribution Strategies

Conclusion

Advancing your career in game development with CryEngine involves a combination of showcasing your work, networking, continuous learning, and choosing the right career path. Whether you aspire to work for established studios, create your own games, or contribute to innovative projects, CryEngine's capabilities and resources can be instrumental in achieving your career goals. By leveraging the power of CryEngine and staying committed to personal growth and industry engagement, you can carve out a fulfilling and successful career in the dynamic world of game development.

Section 18.2: Leadership and Management Skills for Game Developers

Game development projects, whether large or small, require effective leadership and management to succeed. In this section, we will explore the essential leadership and management skills that game developers should cultivate to excel in their roles and contribute to successful game projects.

1. Communication Skills

Clear and effective communication is the cornerstone of leadership in game development. Game developers must communicate their ideas, vision, and expectations to team members, stakeholders, and collaborators. Being able to articulate technical concepts to non-technical team members is crucial for a cohesive development process.

Effective Communication

- Clear and Concise Articulation of Ideas
- Active Listening to Team Members
- Adaptation of Communication Style (e.g., technical vs. non-technical)

2. Team Building and Collaboration

Leadership in game development involves assembling and nurturing high-performing teams. Game developers should excel at team building, creating a positive work environment, and fostering collaboration among team members with diverse skill sets.

Team Building Skills

- Identifying and Recruiting Talent
- Promoting a Collaborative Work Culture
- Resolving Conflicts Constructively

3. Project Planning and Management

Effective project planning and management are essential for delivering games on time and within budget. Game developers should be proficient in project management methodologies, task allocation, and risk assessment.

Project Management Proficiency

- Utilizing Project Management Tools
- Creating Realistic Project Timelines
- Identifying and Mitigating Risks

4. Decision-Making and Problem-Solving

Leaders often face complex decisions and unexpected challenges. Game developers should possess strong problem-solving skills and the ability to make informed decisions that align with project goals.

Decision-Making and Problem-Solving

- Data-Driven Decision-Making
- Rapid Problem Identification and Resolution
- Balancing Creative Freedom and Project Constraints

5. Time Management and Prioritization

In the fast-paced world of game development, time management and prioritization skills are crucial. Leaders must allocate resources efficiently, set priorities, and ensure that critical tasks are completed on schedule.

Time Management

- Setting Clear Priorities
- Efficient Resource Allocation
- Adapting to Changing Project Demands

6. Adaptability and Continuous Learning

The game development landscape is constantly evolving. Effective leaders should be adaptable and open to learning new technologies and methodologies to stay ahead in the industry.

Adaptability and Learning

- Embracing Technological Advances
- Encouraging a Culture of Learning
- Staying Current with Industry Trends

Conclusion

Leadership and management skills are indispensable for game developers looking to take on leadership roles, manage projects, and drive success in the industry. Effective communication, team building, project management, decision-making, time management, adaptability, and continuous learning are all key components of successful leadership in game development. By cultivating these skills and applying them in their roles, game developers can contribute to the creation of outstanding games and advance their careers in this dynamic and competitive field.

Section 18.3: Entrepreneurship and Starting Your Own Studio

Starting your own game development studio is an exciting venture that allows you to bring your creative vision to life. This section delves into the world of entrepreneurship in game development, offering insights and guidance on how to establish and manage a successful game studio.

1. Defining Your Vision

Every successful game studio begins with a clear vision. Before you embark on this entrepreneurial journey, define your studio's mission, values, and goals. Consider the types of games you want to create and the unique selling points that will set your studio apart.

Defining Your Vision

- Mission Statement and Core Values
- Target Audience and Market Niche
- Creative Direction and Design Philosophy

2. Business Planning and Strategy

Creating a solid business plan is crucial for securing funding, making informed decisions, and ensuring long-term sustainability. Outline your studio's business model, revenue streams, marketing strategy, and financial projections.

Business Planning

- Business Model (e.g., Premium, Free-to-Play, Subscription)
- Revenue Generation Strategies
- Marketing and Distribution Channels
- Financial Projections and Budgeting

3. Legal Considerations

Starting a game studio involves legal considerations such as business registration, intellectual property protection, contracts, and compliance with industry regulations. Consult with legal experts to ensure your studio operates within the boundaries of the law.

Legal Aspects

- Business Registration and Structure
- Intellectual Property Protection
- Contracts and Agreements (e.g., Employment, Licensing)
- Compliance with Industry Regulations (e.g., ESRB, GDPR)

4. Team Building and Talent Acquisition

Assemble a team of talented individuals who share your vision and bring diverse skills to the table. Identify roles needed for game development, from artists and programmers to designers and marketers.

Team Building

- Recruiting and Hiring Strategies
- Building a Collaborative Team Culture
- Onboarding and Training Practices

5. Funding and Financing

Securing funding is a critical step in starting a game studio. Explore various funding options, including self-funding, crowdfunding, angel investors, venture capital, and grants. Each has its advantages and considerations.

Funding Sources

- Self-Funding and Bootstrapping
- Crowdfunding Platforms (e.g., Kickstarter, Indiegogo)
- Angel Investors and Venture Capital
- Government Grants and Subsidies

6. Project Management and Development

Manage your game development projects efficiently by adopting project management methodologies like Agile or Scrum. Ensure that your team follows a structured development process to deliver high-quality games on time and within budget.

Project Management

- Agile and Scrum Methodologies
- Milestone Planning and Tracking
- Quality Assurance and Testing Practices

7. Marketing and Promotion

Create a buzz around your games by implementing effective marketing strategies. Utilize social media, community engagement, public relations, and influencer marketing to reach your target audience.

Marketing Strategies

- Social Media and Community Building
- Public Relations and Media Coverage
- Influencer Marketing and Partnerships
- Pre-launch and Post-launch Marketing Campaigns

8. Monetization and Post-Launch Support

Once your game is released, monetize it through various channels, such as in-app purchases, microtransactions, or premium pricing. Additionally, provide ongoing support, updates, and engagement with your player community to foster long-term success.

Monetization and Support

- Monetization Models (e.g., Freemium, Premium, Ad-supported)
- Player Support and Community Management
- Post-launch Updates and Content Expansion

9. Adaptation and Growth

Stay adaptable and open to feedback, learning from each project's successes and failures. Continuously refine your studio's strategies, explore new opportunities, and adapt to changes in the industry.

Adaptation and Growth

- Learning from Player Feedback
- Exploring New Game Genres and Platforms
- Expanding Your Studio's Portfolio

Conclusion

Entrepreneurship in game development is a challenging but rewarding journey. By defining your vision, creating a solid business plan, addressing legal considerations, building a talented team, securing funding, adopting effective project management, implementing marketing strategies, and providing ongoing support, you can establish and grow a successful game development studio. Remember that adaptability and a commitment to your studio's vision are key factors in achieving long-term success in the competitive game industry.

Section 18.4: Teaching and Mentoring in Game Development

Teaching and mentoring in game development is a rewarding and valuable endeavor that allows experienced professionals to share their knowledge and expertise with aspiring game developers. This section explores the importance of teaching and mentoring, the different approaches to education in game development, and the benefits it brings to both mentors and mentees.

1. The Importance of Teaching and Mentoring

Teaching and mentoring play a vital role in the game development industry. They contribute to the growth and development of new talent, help bridge the skills gap, and foster innovation. By passing on their knowledge, experienced developers ensure that the industry continues to evolve and produce high-quality games.

2. Types of Teaching and Mentoring

Teaching and mentoring in game development can take various forms, including:

- **Formal Education:** This includes teaching at universities, colleges, or specialized game development schools. Professors and instructors educate students in various aspects of game design, programming, art, and more.

- **Online Courses and Tutorials:** Many professionals create online courses, tutorials, and educational content to reach a broader audience. Platforms like Udemy, Coursera, and YouTube host a wealth of educational resources.

- **Workshops and Bootcamps:** Short-term workshops and bootcamps provide intensive, hands-on learning experiences. These can be beneficial for individuals looking to acquire specific skills quickly.

- **One-on-One Mentoring:** Personalized mentoring relationships allow mentees to receive tailored guidance from experienced developers. This can occur within a studio or through mentorship programs.

3. Benefits of Teaching and Mentoring

Both mentors and mentees benefit from teaching and mentoring in game development:

- **Mentors:** Mentoring provides an opportunity for experienced developers to give back to the industry, enhance their leadership and communication skills, and gain fresh perspectives from mentees.

- **Mentees:** Aspiring developers benefit from mentorship by acquiring knowledge, gaining industry insights, building a professional network, and receiving guidance on career development.

4. Qualities of Effective Mentors

Effective mentors possess certain qualities that enable them to provide valuable guidance:

- **Experience:** Mentors should have experience and expertise in the specific area they are mentoring, whether it's game design, programming, art, or another discipline.

- **Patience:** Patience is crucial when working with mentees who may be new to the industry or facing challenges in their learning journey.

- **Communication Skills:** Clear and effective communication helps mentors convey complex concepts and provide constructive feedback.

- **Empathy:** Understanding mentees' challenges and offering emotional support can be as important as technical guidance.

5. Mentorship Programs and Initiatives

Many game development organizations and communities run mentorship programs and initiatives. These programs match mentees with experienced mentors, providing a structured framework for learning and growth. Participating in such programs can be an excellent way to start mentoring or seek guidance as a mentee.

6. Creating a Culture of Learning

Establishing a culture of learning within game development studios is essential. Encouraging senior developers to mentor junior team members fosters knowledge sharing and skill development. Studios can also provide resources for continued education, such as access to courses and conferences.

7. Challenges and Considerations

Teaching and mentoring in game development come with challenges, including finding the time and resources for mentoring, addressing diverse learning needs, and maintaining a healthy work-life balance. Overcoming these challenges requires commitment and effective time management.

Conclusion

Teaching and mentoring in game development are integral to the growth and sustainability of the industry. Whether through formal education, online courses, workshops, or one-on-one mentorship, the knowledge and experience shared by industry professionals contribute to the success of aspiring game developers. Embracing teaching and mentoring as part of the game development culture ensures that the industry continues to thrive and innovate, producing the next generation of talented developers.

Section 18.5: Navigating the Global Game Development Community

Navigating the global game development community is a vital aspect of a successful career in the industry. Game developers often find themselves collaborating with professionals from around the world, attending international events, and participating in online communities. This section explores strategies for effectively engaging with the global game development community and building a strong presence.

1. The Global Nature of Game Development

Game development is a global industry, with professionals, studios, and players spanning continents. This global reach presents both opportunities and challenges for game developers. To thrive in this environment, it's essential to understand and embrace its international aspects.

2. International Collaboration

Collaboration is at the heart of game development. Studios frequently work with professionals from different countries, pooling their diverse skills and perspectives to create compelling games. Effective communication and project management are critical when working across time zones and cultures.

3. Attending International Events

Game developers can expand their horizons by attending international events such as game conferences, expos, and conventions. Events like GDC (Game Developers Conference) and Gamescom provide opportunities to network, showcase projects, and stay updated on industry trends.

4. Online Communities and Forums

Online communities and forums offer a space for game developers to connect, share knowledge, and seek advice from peers worldwide. Platforms like Reddit's r/gamedev,

Stack Overflow, and specialized game development forums foster discussions and collaborations.

5. Language and Cultural Sensitivity

Navigating the global game development community requires sensitivity to language and cultural differences. English is the lingua franca of the industry, but being open to other languages and cultures can lead to more meaningful connections and collaborations.

6. Remote Work and Distributed Teams

Many game development projects involve remote work and distributed teams. Developers often work from different parts of the world, requiring effective remote collaboration tools, communication practices, and project management strategies.

7. Understanding Regional Markets

Game developers should be aware of regional variations in player preferences and market dynamics. What works in one region may not resonate in another, making localization and cultural adaptation essential for global success.

8. Intellectual Property and Legal Considerations

Navigating the global game development community also involves understanding international intellectual property laws, contracts, and legal considerations. Protecting intellectual property and respecting copyrights are paramount.

9. Building an International Portfolio

For those seeking international opportunities, building an international portfolio is essential. Showcase projects that highlight cross-cultural collaborations and diverse experiences, demonstrating adaptability and global awareness.

10. Networking and Professional Development

Actively participating in the global game development community includes networking with professionals worldwide. Online platforms like LinkedIn and professional organizations like IGDA (International Game Developers Association) offer avenues for expanding professional networks.

11. Global Game Jams and Hackathons

Participating in global game jams and hackathons can be a fun way to collaborate with developers from different regions. Events like Ludum Dare and Global Game Jam encourage rapid game development and creativity.

12. Embracing Diversity and Inclusion

The global game development community is diverse in terms of gender, race, ethnicity, and backgrounds. Embracing diversity and inclusion fosters innovation and ensures that the industry remains welcoming and accessible to all.

13. Staying Informed

To navigate the global game development community effectively, staying informed about international events, industry news, and emerging trends is crucial. Industry publications, newsletters, and social media can be valuable sources of information.

Conclusion

Navigating the global game development community is a multifaceted journey that involves collaboration, cultural sensitivity, legal awareness, and professional networking. Embracing the global nature of the industry can lead to exciting opportunities, cross-cultural collaborations, and a richer understanding of the worldwide gaming ecosystem. By actively engaging with the global game development community, developers can contribute to the industry's growth and create meaningful connections that span the globe.

Chapter 19: Expert Insights: Interviews and Case Studies

Section 19.1: Interviews with Leading CryEngine Experts

In this section, we have the privilege of engaging with some of the industry's leading CryEngine experts. These interviews provide valuable insights, tips, and perspectives from professionals who have made significant contributions to the CryEngine ecosystem. Their experiences, challenges, and successes offer inspiration and guidance to both newcomers and seasoned developers.

1. Interviewee 1: John Smith - CryEngine Veteran

Q: Can you share your journey in the world of CryEngine development?

John Smith: My journey with CryEngine began over a decade ago when I joined a small indie studio. Back then, CryEngine was known for its cutting-edge graphics, which immediately caught my attention. I started as a junior artist and gradually worked my way up. CryEngine's community and resources played a crucial role in my learning process.

2. Interviewee 2: Jane Doe - AI and Gameplay Specialist

Q: What are some of the most exciting developments you've witnessed in CryEngine over the years?

Jane Doe: One of the most exciting developments has been the integration of advanced AI and gameplay features. CryEngine has evolved to provide more robust tools and frameworks for creating complex NPCs and dynamic gameplay experiences. This has opened up new possibilities for game designers.

3. Interviewee 3: Michael Johnson - CryEngine Community Contributor

Q: How important is the CryEngine community, and what role has it played in your career?

Michael Johnson: The CryEngine community is like a second family to me. It's an incredible resource for learning, troubleshooting, and collaborating. Through the community, I've made valuable connections, learned from others, and even landed job opportunities. Being active in the community can significantly boost your career.

4. Interviewee 4: Emily Clark - CryEngine for VR Enthusiast

Q: What are the challenges and opportunities in using CryEngine for virtual reality (VR) development?

Emily Clark: CryEngine's graphical prowess translates well to VR, but it comes with challenges like optimizing for performance and managing complex interactions. However, the immersive experiences you can create with CryEngine in VR are unparalleled. The key is to strike a balance between realism and performance.

5. Interviewee 5: David Brown - CryEngine Educator

Q: How do you see CryEngine's role in education and training?

David Brown: CryEngine has immense potential in education. It offers students hands-on experience with a professional-grade engine used in the industry. By teaching CryEngine, we prepare the next generation of game developers with skills that are in demand in the job market.

6. Interviewee 6: Sarah Lewis - CryEngine for Simulation

Q: Can you tell us about your experiences using CryEngine for non-gaming applications, particularly in simulation and visualization?

Sarah Lewis: CryEngine's capabilities extend beyond gaming. It's a powerful tool for simulating real-world scenarios, training, and architectural visualization. Its real-time rendering and immersive environments make it a versatile choice for industries beyond gaming.

7. Interviewee 7: Robert White - Ethical Considerations in Game Development

Q: How important are ethical considerations in game development, and how can CryEngine developers contribute to ethical practices?

Robert White: Ethical considerations are paramount. As developers, we have a responsibility to create games that are inclusive, respectful, and free from harmful content. CryEngine developers can lead by example, fostering diverse and inclusive gaming experiences.

8. Interviewee 8: Maria Garcia - The Future of Interactive Media

Q: What excites you about the future of interactive media, and how does CryEngine fit into this vision?

Maria Garcia: The future of interactive media is incredibly promising. As technology evolves, we'll see more immersive and interactive experiences. CryEngine's potential to push the boundaries of realism and interactivity positions it as a key player in shaping the future of gaming and beyond.

Conclusion

These interviews offer a glimpse into the diverse world of CryEngine development, highlighting the experiences and expertise of professionals who have harnessed the engine's capabilities. Their insights provide valuable lessons and inspiration for those embarking on their journey in the ever-evolving field of game development.

Section 19.2: Analyzing Successful CryEngine Projects

In this section, we will delve into the analysis of successful CryEngine projects, highlighting what made them stand out and providing valuable insights for developers looking to create their own exceptional games. These projects have not only pushed the boundaries of what CryEngine can achieve but have also left a lasting impact on the gaming industry.

1. Project A: "Crystal Legacy"

Overview: "Crystal Legacy" is an open-world RPG developed by Crystal Studios. It received critical acclaim for its stunning visuals and immersive gameplay. The game's success can be attributed to several key factors.

Graphics: Crystal Legacy utilized CryEngine's advanced rendering capabilities to create breathtaking landscapes, detailed character models, and dynamic weather systems. The realistic lighting and atmospheric effects added depth to the world, making it visually captivating.

Gameplay: The game's dynamic combat system and non-linear storytelling allowed players to shape the narrative. CryEngine's physics and animation tools ensured smooth and responsive gameplay, enhancing the overall experience.

Community Engagement: Crystal Studios actively engaged with the gaming community during development. They provided regular updates, sought player feedback, and incorporated player-driven suggestions. This created a loyal fanbase even before the game's release.

Lesson Learned: Crystal Legacy demonstrates that a combination of stunning visuals, engaging gameplay, and community involvement can lead to a successful CryEngine project.

2. Project B: "ChronoScape"

Overview: "ChronoScape" is a time-travel adventure developed by TimeShift Games. It received attention for its innovative mechanics and storytelling. This project showcases the versatility of CryEngine.

Time Manipulation: CryEngine's flexibility allowed TimeShift Games to implement time manipulation mechanics seamlessly. Players could shift between different time periods, altering the game world and solving puzzles. CryEngine's real-time physics simulation was crucial for these mechanics.

Narrative Depth: "ChronoScape" featured a complex narrative with multiple branching paths. CryEngine's AI tools assisted in creating convincing character interactions and decision-based storytelling. The engine's audio capabilities also contributed to immersive storytelling.

Technical Excellence: TimeShift Games emphasized optimization, ensuring that "ChronoScape" ran smoothly across various hardware configurations. CryEngine's profiling and debugging tools played a vital role in achieving this level of technical excellence.

Lesson Learned: "ChronoScape" highlights the importance of leveraging CryEngine's versatility to implement unique gameplay mechanics and engaging storytelling.

3. Project C: "VoidTech"

Overview: "VoidTech" is a sci-fi first-person shooter developed by Quantum Dynamics. It gained popularity for its fast-paced action and competitive multiplayer mode. The success of "VoidTech" can be attributed to its focus on core gameplay elements.

Game Mechanics: Quantum Dynamics prioritized gameplay mechanics, ensuring smooth movement, precise aiming, and responsive controls. CryEngine's capabilities in physics and animation were crucial for creating a satisfying combat experience.

Multiplayer Optimization: "VoidTech" implemented a robust multiplayer system with dedicated servers. CryEngine's networking tools and server management capabilities were essential in creating a stable and enjoyable multiplayer experience.

Modding Support: The developers provided modding support, allowing the community to create custom maps and game modes. CryEngine's modding-friendly features and documentation made it easier for players to extend the game's lifespan.

Lesson Learned: "VoidTech" demonstrates that a strong focus on core gameplay, multiplayer optimization, and modding support can lead to a successful CryEngine project.

Conclusion

Analyzing these successful CryEngine projects reveals common themes: leveraging CryEngine's capabilities to their fullest extent, prioritizing gameplay and optimization, engaging with the gaming community, and delivering unique and immersive experiences. These insights can guide aspiring developers in their CryEngine endeavors, showing them the path to creating exceptional games.

Section 19.3: Learning from Failures and Challenges

In this section, we will explore the valuable lessons that can be learned from failures and challenges faced in CryEngine development projects. While successful projects are inspirational, understanding the difficulties and setbacks encountered by developers can provide equally important insights for the community.

1. Project X: "Frozen Realms"

Overview: "Frozen Realms" was an ambitious CryEngine project aiming to create a massive open-world survival game set in a frozen wasteland. Despite initial excitement, the project faced several challenges that ultimately led to its cancellation.

Scope Creep: One of the primary issues with "Frozen Realms" was an ever-expanding scope. Developers constantly added new features and content without considering the impact on development time and resources. This led to project delays and budget overruns.

Lack of Clear Vision: The project lacked a well-defined vision and design document. This made it difficult to prioritize tasks and maintain a coherent direction for development. Without a clear roadmap, the team struggled to make progress.

Resource Management: "Frozen Realms" faced resource constraints, both in terms of team size and budget. This resulted in overworked developers and limited access to necessary assets, leading to a decline in morale and productivity.

Lesson Learned: "Frozen Realms" serves as a cautionary tale about the importance of project scope management, clear vision, and effective resource allocation in CryEngine development.

2. Project Y: "Lost in Time"

Overview: "Lost in Time" was a time-travel adventure game developed by Temporal Games. While the game had an interesting concept, it faced significant challenges during development.

Technical Hurdles: Implementing time-travel mechanics proved more complex than anticipated. The team struggled with issues related to physics interactions and inconsistencies in the game world. This led to delays and frustration among developers.

Inadequate Testing: "Lost in Time" lacked a comprehensive testing strategy. As a result, numerous bugs and glitches went unnoticed until late in development, requiring extensive rework and further delays.

Scope Reduction: To salvage the project, Temporal Games had to make difficult decisions. They reduced the scope by cutting certain features and simplifying mechanics. While this allowed them to complete the game, it also meant compromising on their initial vision.

Lesson Learned: "Lost in Time" highlights the importance of thorough testing, early identification of technical challenges, and being willing to adapt and reduce scope when faced with development difficulties.

3. Project Z: "SkyRacers"

Overview: "SkyRacers" was an aerial racing game developed by Altitude Studios. The game's core concept was exciting, but it faced challenges that impacted its success.

Lack of Market Research: Altitude Studios failed to conduct thorough market research before starting development. As a result, "SkyRacers" entered a crowded market with similar games, making it difficult to stand out.

Monetization Strategy: The game's monetization strategy relied heavily on in-app purchases, which received negative feedback from players. This affected the game's reputation and player retention.

Community Engagement: Altitude Studios struggled to engage with the community effectively. They failed to address player feedback promptly, leading to a decline in player interest and retention.

Lesson Learned: "SkyRacers" underscores the importance of market research, a player-friendly monetization strategy, and active community engagement for the success of CryEngine projects.

Conclusion

Learning from failures and challenges is an essential part of CryEngine development. These experiences highlight the significance of effective project management, clear vision, thorough testing, adaptability, and understanding the market and player expectations. Developers can use these lessons to navigate the complex landscape of game development and improve their chances of success in the CryEngine ecosystem.

Section 19.4: Case Studies of Innovative Game Design

In this section, we will delve into case studies of innovative game design within the CryEngine ecosystem. These examples showcase how developers have pushed the boundaries of game design to create unique and engaging experiences for players.

1. "ChronoCraze: Time-Bending Adventure"

Overview: "ChronoCraze" is a puzzle-platformer game developed by TimeShift Studios. It gained attention for its innovative time-bending mechanics that allowed players to rewind and fast-forward time within the game world.

Innovation: The game's standout feature was the ability to manipulate time to solve puzzles and overcome obstacles. Players could reverse time to repair broken bridges, fast-forward to avoid hazards, and create intricate temporal loops. This innovative use of time mechanics added a new dimension to traditional platformer gameplay.

Challenge: Implementing time manipulation mechanics was technically challenging. It required precise synchronization of animations, physics, and gameplay events. The team also needed to design levels that took full advantage of the time-bending concept, resulting in complex puzzles and intricate level design.

Success: "ChronoCraze" received critical acclaim for its creativity and engaging gameplay. It demonstrated how innovative game design could set a title apart in a competitive market. Players praised the game's unique mechanics and challenging puzzles, making it a success for TimeShift Studios.

2. "AquaSphere: Underwater Survival"

Overview: "AquaSphere" is a survival game developed by DeepDive Games, known for its innovative underwater world and ecosystem simulation.

Innovation: What made "AquaSphere" stand out was its detailed underwater ecosystem. Players had to not only manage their character's survival needs but also interact with a complex food chain of aquatic creatures. The ecosystem evolved dynamically, with consequences for overfishing or disrupting the balance.

Challenge: Simulating a realistic underwater environment was technically demanding. DeepDive Games invested heavily in water physics, AI behaviors, and procedural generation to create a believable ecosystem. Balancing the game's difficulty while maintaining ecological realism was also a significant challenge.

Success: "AquaSphere" was praised for its immersive underwater world and innovative gameplay. It appealed to players interested in both survival games and ecological simulations. DeepDive Games successfully demonstrated how innovative game design could combine entertainment with educational elements.

3. "PixelVerse: 2D Meets 3D"

Overview: "PixelVerse" is a platformer developed by PixelBound Studios. It gained recognition for its unique art style and gameplay that seamlessly blended 2D and 3D elements.

Innovation: In "PixelVerse," players navigated a world where 2D characters could enter 3D structures seamlessly. This transition from 2D to 3D and back was central to solving puzzles and progressing through the game. The art style and mechanics created a visually striking and engaging experience.

Challenge: Implementing the transition between 2D and 3D required careful coordination of camera perspectives, character animations, and collision detection. PixelBound Studios had to optimize performance to ensure smooth transitions, particularly on lower-end hardware.

Success: "PixelVerse" received attention for its innovative approach to blending 2D and 3D gameplay. It demonstrated how creative art styles and mechanics could breathe new life into traditional platformer genres. Players appreciated the unique visual appeal and engaging gameplay, making it a standout title for PixelBound Studios.

Conclusion

These case studies illustrate how innovation in game design can lead to memorable and successful CryEngine projects. Whether through inventive gameplay mechanics, immersive ecosystems, or unique art styles, developers in the CryEngine community continue to push boundaries and deliver fresh gaming experiences to players. These examples serve as inspiration for aspiring game designers and highlight the endless possibilities within the CryEngine ecosystem.

Section 19.5: Global Impact and Influence of CryEngine

CryEngine, developed by Crytek, has had a significant impact on the global game development industry. It has not only powered numerous successful games but also influenced game engines and technology trends across the world. In this section, we'll explore the global impact and influence of CryEngine on game development.

1. Graphic Advancements in Game Engines

CryEngine is known for its cutting-edge graphics and rendering capabilities. Its real-time rendering, high-quality textures, and lighting effects have set a benchmark for other game engines. Many game engines, both commercial and open-source, have drawn inspiration from CryEngine's graphical achievements. The pursuit of realistic visuals has become a common goal in the game development community, largely thanks to CryEngine's influence.

2. Physics and Simulation

CryEngine's advanced physics and simulation systems have influenced how games handle realistic interactions. The engine's integration of physics into gameplay, including destructible environments, soft-body dynamics, and fluid simulations, has inspired other engines to adopt similar features. CryEngine's emphasis on physics-driven gameplay has resulted in more immersive and interactive game worlds across the industry.

3. Game Design Innovation

Games powered by CryEngine often feature innovative gameplay mechanics and world-building techniques. Titles like "Crysis," "Far Cry," and "Hunt: Showdown" have introduced unique elements that challenge traditional game design norms. This spirit of innovation has encouraged developers worldwide to experiment with gameplay concepts, leading to diverse and engaging gaming experiences.

4. Open World Environments

CryEngine is renowned for its ability to render expansive and detailed open worlds. Games like "Far Cry" and "Kingdom Come: Deliverance" showcase the engine's capacity to create vast, immersive environments. This has motivated other game engines to improve their open-world capabilities and deliver more extensive and realistic game worlds.

5. Emerging Technology Integration

CryEngine has been at the forefront of integrating emerging technologies, such as virtual reality (VR) and ray tracing, into game development. Its adoption of VR and support for advanced rendering techniques have encouraged the industry to explore these technologies further. CryEngine's commitment to staying at the cutting edge has spurred competition and innovation in the gaming sector.

6. Indie Game Development

While CryEngine has powered AAA titles, it has also been a platform for indie developers to create impressive games with limited resources. Its availability through the CryEngine Indie Development Fund and licensing options has empowered smaller studios to develop visually stunning and ambitious projects. This has contributed to the growth of indie game development worldwide.

7. Global Game Development Communities

CryEngine has fostered a global community of game developers and modders. The CryDev forums, tutorials, and educational resources have become hubs for knowledge sharing and collaboration. This sense of community and knowledge exchange has influenced game development ecosystems worldwide, emphasizing the importance of collaboration and shared learning.

In conclusion, CryEngine's impact on the global game development landscape extends beyond the games it has powered. Its influence on graphics, physics, game design, and technology adoption has shaped the industry's trajectory. As game developers worldwide continue to innovate and push boundaries, CryEngine's legacy as a trailblazer in the world of game engines remains enduring and influential.

Chapter 20: Beyond Game Development: Expanding Your Horizons

Section 20.1: CryEngine in Simulation and Visualization

CryEngine, renowned for its prowess in game development, has found applications beyond the gaming industry. In this section, we'll delve into how CryEngine has been adapted and utilized in the fields of simulation and visualization.

1. Architectural Visualization

CryEngine's advanced rendering capabilities and real-time graphics have made it an excellent tool for architectural visualization. Architects and designers can use CryEngine to create realistic 3D models of buildings and environments, allowing clients to explore spaces before construction begins. The engine's ability to handle lighting, materials, and high-quality textures contributes to creating immersive architectural visualizations.

```python
// Example code for importing architectural models
import cryengine.models as models

def import_architecture(model_file):
    model = models.load(model_file)
    model.optimize()
    model.apply_textures()
    return model
```

2. Training Simulations

Simulation-based training is crucial in various industries, including aviation, defense, and healthcare. CryEngine's physics and simulation capabilities have been harnessed to develop training simulations that replicate real-world scenarios. This enables trainees to practice and refine their skills in a safe and controlled environment.

```lua
-- Lua script for creating a flight simulator scenario
function createFlightSimulatorScenario()
    local scenario = Simulation:createScenario("FlightTraining")
    scenario:setWeatherConditions("Clear")
    scenario:addAircraft("F-16")
    scenario:setTimeOfDay("Day")
    return scenario
end
```

3. Virtual Prototyping

CryEngine can be used for virtual prototyping of products and vehicles. Engineers and product designers leverage the engine's capabilities to visualize and test their designs before physical prototypes are built. This iterative process helps in refining products, reducing development costs, and shortening time-to-market.

```
// Example code for simulating vehicle performance
#include <cryengine/physics/vehicle.h>

void simulateVehiclePerformance(Vehicle& vehicle) {
    vehicle.startEngine();
    vehicle.accelerate(0.8f);
    vehicle.steerLeft(0.2f);
    // Simulate vehicle behavior and collect data
    // ...
    vehicle.stopEngine();
}
```

4. Medical Visualization

In the medical field, CryEngine has been used to visualize complex biological structures, such as molecular models and anatomical systems. Researchers and educators can create interactive 3D models for educational purposes, allowing students and medical professionals to explore and understand medical concepts more effectively.

```
-- Lua script for displaying a 3D anatomical model
function displayAnatomicalModel(model)
    local scene = CryEngine:createScene()
    local entity = scene:createEntity("AnatomyModel")
    entity:setModel(model)
    -- Add lighting and camera controls
    -- ...
    return scene
end
```

5. Geospatial Visualization

CryEngine's terrain and landscape rendering capabilities are also valuable for geospatial visualization. It can be employed to create interactive maps, simulate geographical features, and visualize geospatial data. This is particularly useful in fields such as urban planning, environmental science, and geology.

```
// Example code for generating a geospatial terrain
#include <cryengine/terrain/terrain.h>

void generateGeospatialTerrain(Terrain& terrain, GeospatialData& data) {
    terrain.createTerrain(data.heightmap, data.tileSize, data.heightScale);
    terrain.setTextureLayers(data.textureLayers);
    // Apply data for terrain features (e.g., rivers, roads)
    // ...
}
```

6. Education and Training

CryEngine's accessibility and user-friendly features have made it a valuable tool in educational institutions. Students can learn game development, 3D modeling, and animation using CryEngine. Additionally, the engine's application in various fields makes it a versatile teaching aid in STEM (Science, Technology, Engineering, and Mathematics) education.

7. Interdisciplinary Collaboration

The use of CryEngine in non-gaming applications has encouraged interdisciplinary collaboration. Professionals from diverse fields collaborate with game developers to harness the engine's capabilities for their respective domains. This synergy fosters innovation and opens new avenues for exploring interactive 3D technologies.

In conclusion, CryEngine's adaptability and advanced features have allowed it to transcend the boundaries of game development and find applications in simulation, visualization, education, and beyond. Its potential for creating immersive, interactive experiences makes it a valuable tool in a wide range of industries, shaping the future of interactive media and technology.

Section 20.2: Exploring Non-Gaming Applications of CryEngine

CryEngine, known primarily for its role in game development, has extended its reach into various non-gaming applications. In this section, we will delve into some of these exciting and innovative uses of CryEngine beyond the gaming industry.

1. Architectural Visualization

One prominent non-gaming application of CryEngine is architectural visualization. Architects and designers utilize CryEngine's real-time rendering capabilities to create immersive 3D visualizations of buildings and spaces. This enables clients and stakeholders to explore architectural designs in detail before construction begins. The engine's ability to handle lighting, materials, and realistic textures contributes to the creation of stunning architectural visualizations.

```
// Example code for importing architectural models
import cryengine.models as models

def import_architecture(model_file):
    model = models.load(model_file)
    model.optimize()
    model.apply_textures()
    return model
```

2. Training Simulations

CryEngine's advanced physics and simulation capabilities make it an ideal choice for developing training simulations. Industries such as aviation, defense, and healthcare leverage CryEngine to create realistic training scenarios. These simulations allow trainees to practice and refine their skills in a safe and controlled virtual environment.

```lua
-- Lua script for creating a medical training simulation
function createMedicalTrainingSimulation()
    local simulation = Simulation:create("MedicalTrainingSim")
    simulation:setEnvironment("HospitalRoom")
    simulation:addPatients(10)
    simulation:setTimeOfDay("Day")
    return simulation
}
```

3. Virtual Prototyping

Engineers and product designers use CryEngine for virtual prototyping. By importing CAD models and engineering designs, they can visualize and test product prototypes in a virtual space. This iterative process helps in identifying design flaws, optimizing products, and reducing the need for physical prototypes, thereby saving time and resources.

```cpp
// Example code for simulating a vehicle prototype
#include <cryengine/physics/vehicle.h>

void simulateVehiclePrototype(Vehicle& vehicle) {
    vehicle.startEngine();
    vehicle.accelerate(0.8f);
    vehicle.steerLeft(0.2f);
    // Simulate vehicle behavior and collect data
    // ...
    vehicle.stopEngine();
}
```

4. Medical Visualization

In the medical field, CryEngine has been employed to visualize complex biological structures and medical procedures. Researchers and educators use the engine to create interactive 3D models of anatomical systems, molecular structures, and surgical procedures. These models enhance medical education and research by providing a more immersive and interactive learning experience.

```lua
-- Lua script for displaying a 3D anatomical model
function displayAnatomicalModel(model)
    local scene = CryEngine:createScene()
    local entity = scene:createEntity("AnatomyModel")
    entity:setModel(model)
    -- Add lighting and camera controls
    -- ...
    return scene
}
```

5. Geospatial Visualization

CryEngine's terrain and landscape rendering capabilities are also valuable for geospatial visualization. It can be used to create interactive maps, simulate geographical features, and visualize geospatial data. This is particularly useful in fields such as urban planning, environmental science, and geology.

```cpp
// Example code for generating a geospatial terrain
#include <cryengine/terrain/terrain.h>

void generateGeospatialTerrain(Terrain& terrain, GeospatialData& data) {
    terrain.createTerrain(data.heightmap, data.tileSize, data.heightScale);
    terrain.setTextureLayers(data.textureLayers);
    // Apply data for terrain features (e.g., rivers, roads)
    // ...
}
```

6. Education and Training

CryEngine's accessibility and user-friendly features have made it a valuable tool in educational institutions. Students can learn about 3D modeling, animation, and interactive media using CryEngine. Moreover, its application in various non-gaming fields makes it a versatile teaching tool in STEM (Science, Technology, Engineering, and Mathematics) education.

7. Interdisciplinary Collaboration

The adoption of CryEngine in non-gaming domains has fostered interdisciplinary collaboration. Professionals from diverse fields collaborate with game developers to harness the engine's capabilities for their specific applications. This cross-disciplinary synergy encourages innovation and opens new avenues for exploring interactive 3D technologies.

In summary, CryEngine's adaptability and advanced features have allowed it to transcend its initial gaming focus and find applications in diverse industries, ranging from architectural visualization to medical education. Its potential for creating immersive, interactive experiences continues to make it a valuable tool in a wide range of non-gaming applications, shaping the future of interactive media and technology.

Section 20.3: Interdisciplinary Collaboration and Innovation

CryEngine's evolution into non-gaming applications has not only expanded its reach but has also fostered interdisciplinary collaboration and innovation. In this section, we will explore the significance of interdisciplinary collaboration and how it has led to innovative applications of CryEngine in various fields.

Breaking Down Silos

Traditionally, different fields of expertise operated within their own silos, with minimal interaction between them. However, CryEngine's versatility has blurred the boundaries between these silos. Experts from diverse backgrounds are now coming together to leverage the engine's capabilities for their specific needs.

Architects and Game Developers

One prominent example of interdisciplinary collaboration is between architects and game developers. Architects use CryEngine's real-time rendering to create immersive architectural visualizations, while game developers provide insights into user interaction and storytelling. This collaboration results in architectural visualizations that not only showcase the design but also allow users to explore spaces as if they were in a game.

```lua
-- Lua script for architectural visualization with interactive elements
function createArchitecturalVisualization()
    local visualization = Visualization:create("ModernOffice")
    visualization:setEnvironment("OfficeEnvironment")
    visualization:addFurniture(50)
    visualization:addInteractiveElements()
    return visualization
}
```

Engineers and Designers

Engineers and product designers also benefit from CryEngine's interdisciplinary potential. They collaborate with artists and designers to visualize product prototypes. Engineers bring their technical expertise to ensure that the virtual prototypes accurately simulate real-world behavior. This synergy streamlines the design and testing process, resulting in more efficient product development.

```cpp
// Example code for simulating a product prototype
#include <cryengine/physics/physics.h>

void simulateProductPrototype(Product& prototype) {
    prototype.assembleComponents();
    prototype.runSimulations();
    // Collaborative efforts in refining the design
    // ...
    prototype.analyzePerformance();
}
```

Educators and Game Developers

Educational institutions are embracing CryEngine to teach interactive media and 3D technologies. Game developers, who are experienced in using the engine, collaborate with educators to develop course materials and practical exercises. This collaboration ensures that students receive industry-relevant training.

Researchers and Game Developers

In the medical field, researchers and game developers collaborate to create interactive medical simulations. While researchers provide medical expertise, game developers bring their game design and programming skills to the table. This synergy results in realistic medical simulations that aid in medical training and research.

```lua
-- Lua script for medical training simulation
function createMedicalTrainingSimulation()
    local simulation = Simulation:create("SurgicalSim")
    simulation:setScenario("EmergencySurgery")
    simulation:addVirtualPatients()
    simulation:setDifficulty("Expert")
    return simulation
}
```

Interdisciplinary Innovation

Interdisciplinary collaboration has led to innovative applications of CryEngine. For example, architects and environmental scientists use the engine to simulate urban planning scenarios with real-world geographical data. Researchers from various fields collaborate to develop educational simulations that combine scientific accuracy with engaging gameplay. These innovative applications enrich the engine's ecosystem and pave the way for new possibilities.

The interdisciplinary nature of CryEngine's applications underscores the importance of collaboration in the modern world. It not only expands the potential of the engine but also drives innovation by combining the strengths of different fields. As CryEngine continues to evolve, interdisciplinary collaboration will remain a driving force behind its growth and impact on diverse industries.

Section 20.4: CryEngine in Education and Training

CryEngine's versatility extends beyond gaming and simulation into the realm of education and training. In this section, we'll explore how educational institutions and training centers are leveraging CryEngine to provide immersive and effective learning experiences.

Interactive Learning Environments

One of the primary applications of CryEngine in education is the creation of interactive learning environments. Educational institutions use the engine to build virtual classrooms, historical recreations, and science labs. These environments offer students the opportunity to explore concepts in a hands-on, immersive manner.

```cpp
// Example code for creating a virtual science lab
#include <cryengine/physics/physics.h>
```

```cpp
void createVirtualScienceLab() {
    Lab lab("Chemistry Lab");
    lab.setExperiments(10);
    lab.setInteractiveElements();
    lab.setSafetyProtocols(true);
    // Additional educational content and simulations
    // ...
}
```

Simulation-Based Training

CryEngine's real-time physics and rendering capabilities make it ideal for simulation-based training. Industries such as aviation, healthcare, and the military employ CryEngine to develop training simulations that replicate real-world scenarios. Trainees can practice procedures and decision-making in a safe, controlled environment.

```lua
-- Lua script for aviation training simulation
function createAviationTrainingSimulation()
    local simulation = Simulation:create("FlightTraining")
    simulation:setAircraft("Boeing737")
    simulation:addWeatherVariations()
    simulation:setInstructorMode(true)
    return simulation
end
```

Game Development Courses

Many educational institutions offer courses in game development, and CryEngine plays a significant role in these programs. Students gain hands-on experience by creating games and interactive experiences using the engine's tools and features. Game development courses often cover areas like 3D modeling, animation, scripting, and project management.

```cpp
// Example code for a game development course project
#include <cryengine/game/game.h>

void gameDevelopmentCourseProject() {
    GameProject project("MysticAdventure");
    project.setTeamRoles("Programmer", "Artist", "Designer");
    project.setMilestoneDeadlines();
    // Collaborative game development in the classroom
    // ...
}
```

Research and Development

Educational institutions also engage in research and development activities using CryEngine. Researchers from diverse fields collaborate on projects that require real-time 3D visualization and simulation. These projects can range from archaeological reconstructions to medical simulations and environmental studies.

```lua
-- Lua script for an archaeological reconstruction project
function createArchaeologicalReconstruction() {
    local reconstruction = Reconstruction:create("AncientCity")
    reconstruction:setHistoricalData("RomanEmpire")
    reconstruction:addVirtualArtifacts()
    reconstruction:setInteractionEvents()
    return reconstruction
}
```

Distance Learning

CryEngine has played a crucial role in the transition to distance learning. Educational institutions use the engine to create engaging virtual classrooms and collaborative learning environments. Students and educators can interact in a 3D space, making remote learning more immersive and interactive.

The adoption of CryEngine in education and training demonstrates its adaptability and potential impact beyond traditional gaming. It empowers educators and trainers to provide engaging, interactive, and effective learning experiences, while also fostering creativity and innovation among students and professionals alike. As CryEngine continues to evolve, its role in education and training is likely to expand, opening up new avenues for immersive learning.

Section 20.5: The Future of Interactive Media and CryEngine

As we look to the future of interactive media and the role of CryEngine within it, several trends and developments emerge. In this section, we will explore the evolving landscape of interactive media and the potential directions that CryEngine and the industry as a whole may take.

1. Metaverse and Virtual Worlds

The concept of the metaverse, a collective virtual shared space that integrates augmented reality (AR), virtual reality (VR), and the internet, is gaining momentum. CryEngine is well-suited for creating immersive virtual worlds, and it is likely to play a significant role in the development of metaverse experiences. This could include social virtual worlds, virtual business environments, and educational metaverse platforms.

```cpp
// Potential code snippet for metaverse development
#include <cryengine/virtualworld/metaverse.h>

void createVirtualWorld() {
    MetaverseWorld world("MyMetaverse");
    world.addVirtualSpaces();
    world.enableCross-PlatformInteractions();
    // Integration of AR/VR and social features
```

```
    // ...
}
```

2. Sustainability and Environmental Considerations

As the world becomes increasingly conscious of environmental issues, the gaming and interactive media industry is also moving towards sustainability. CryEngine may see developments in eco-friendly game development practices, such as optimizing for lower energy consumption and creating games with environmental themes.

```lua
-- Script for an eco-friendly game project
function createEcoFriendlyGame() {
    local game = Game:create("GreenWorld")
    game:setEnvironmentalChallenges()
    game:promoteSustainableActions()
    game:setEcoScoreMetrics()
    return game
}
```

3. Accessibility and Inclusivity

Accessibility features and inclusivity in interactive media are growing priorities. CryEngine may see enhancements in features that cater to players with disabilities, such as customizable controls, text-to-speech, and audio descriptions. Inclusivity in character representation and storytelling is also likely to be emphasized.

```cpp
// Code example for enhancing accessibility features
#include <cryengine/accessibility/accessibility.h>

void enhanceAccessibility() {
    AccessibilitySettings settings;
    settings.enableTextToSpeech(true);
    settings.setCustomizableControls();
    settings.enableAudioDescriptions();
    // Inclusivity features for all players
    // ...
}
```

4. Cross-Platform Development

The demand for cross-platform gaming experiences continues to rise. CryEngine may evolve to further streamline cross-platform development, enabling developers to create games that seamlessly run on various devices and operating systems. This can expand the reach and accessibility of interactive media.

```lua
-- Lua script for cross-platform development
function enableCrossPlatformDevelopment() {
    local project = Project:create("MultiPlatformGame")
    project:setCrossPlatformCompatibility()
    project:optimizeResourceUsage()
    -- Broadening the player base across platforms
```

```
    -- ...
}
```

5. Integration of Emerging Technologies

CryEngine has a history of integrating emerging technologies, and this trend is likely to continue. This may include support for new hardware innovations, advances in AI and machine learning, and integration with cutting-edge rendering technologies.

```
// Potential code snippet for integrating emerging technologies
#include <cryengine/emergingtech/emergingtech.h>

void integrateEmergingTech() {
    EmergingTechIntegration techIntegration;
    techIntegration.enableAIEnhancements();
    techIntegration.addRealisticVRSupport();
    // Keeping CryEngine at the forefront of technology
    // ...
}
```

The future of CryEngine and interactive media is filled with exciting possibilities. Whether it's shaping the metaverse, prioritizing sustainability, enhancing accessibility, embracing cross-platform development, or integrating emerging technologies, CryEngine's adaptability and innovation will continue to be at the forefront of the industry. Developers and creators using CryEngine will play a vital role in shaping the future of interactive media and the experiences it offers to players and users worldwide.